FLORENTINE CODEX

Florentine Codex

General History of the Things of New Spain

FRAY BERNARDINO DE SAHAGÚN

Book 1 – The Gods

Translated from the Aztec into English, with notes and illustrations
(Second edition, revised)

By

Arthur J. O. Anderson
School of American Research

Charles E. Dibble
University of Utah

IN THIRTEEN PARTS

PART II

Chapter heading designs are from the Codex

Published by
The School of American Research and The University of Utah

Monographs of The School of American Research
Santa Fe, New Mexico

Number 14, Part II 1970

Second edition, revised

First paperback edition 2012

ISBN: 978-1-60781-157-2 (BOOK 1)
ISBN: 978-1-60781-192-3 (SET)

Published and distributed by
The University of Utah Press
Salt Lake City, Utah

CONTENTS

FIRST BOOK. HERE ARE NAMED THE GODS WHOM THE NATIVES WORSHIPPED

LIST OF ILLUSTRATIONS

BOOK I

following page 32

De los Dioses

FIRST BOOK. HERE ARE NAMED THE GODS WHOM THE NATIVES WORSHIPPED.

INIC CE AMUXTLI, VNCAN MOTENEOA, IN TETEUH: IN QUJNMOTEUTIAIA IN NICAN TLACA.

First Chapter, which telleth of the highest of the gods[1] whom they worshipped and to whom they offered sacrifices in ancient times.

Uitzilopochtli (Hummingbird from the Left)[2] was only a common man, just a man,[3] a sorcerer, an omen of evil; a madman, a deceiver,[4] a creator of war, a war-lord, an instigator of war.

For it was said of him that he brought hunger and plague — that is, war.[5] And when a feast day was celebrated,[6] captives were slain; ceremonially bathed slaves were offered up. The merchants bathed them.[7]

Jnic ce capitulo, yntechpa tlatoa, yn oc cenca tlapanauja teteuh: yn qujnmoteutiaia, yoan yn qujntlamanjliaia, yn ie vecauh.

Vitzilubuchtli: çan maceoalli, çan tlacatl catca: naoalli, tetzaujtl, atlacacemelle, teixcuepanj: qujiocoianj in iaoiutl, iaotecanj, iaotlatoanj:

ca itechpa mjtoaia, tepan qujtlaça yn xiuhcoatl, in mamalhoaztli. q. n. iaoiutl, teuatl, tlachinolli. Auh yn jquac ilhujqujxtiloia, malmjcoaia, tlaaltilmjcoaia: tealtiaia, yn pochteca.

---

1. The corresponding Spanish text of the *Florentine Codex* reads: *"capitulo primero, que habla, del principal dios. . . ."*

2. Ángel María Garibay K., *Historia de la Literatura Náhuatl* (Mexico: Editorial Porrúa, S. A., 1953–54), Vol. II, p. 404: "Huitzilopochtli, *nombre del numen principal de Tenochtitlan. El nombre significa* Precioso Izquierdero *y se aplica al sol. En la concepción cósmica del antiguo mexicano el dios quedaba al Sur, que es la izquierda del mundo, ya que el camino del sol es Oriente a Poniente."*

3. Eduard Seler, in *Gesammelte Abhandlungen zur Amerikanischen Sprach-und Alterthumskunde* (Berlin: A. Asher & Co., 1902–23), Vol. II, p. 423, refers to him as *nur ein Stammheros.*

4. Eduard Seler, in *Einige Kapitel aus dem Geschichtswerk des Fray Bernardino de Sahagun aus dem Aztekischen wortgetreu übersetzt* (Caecelie Seler-Sachs, Walter Lehmann, Walter Krickeberg, eds.; Stuttgart: Stecker und Schroeder, 1927), p. 1, thus phrases the passage: *"Uitzilopochtli war nur ein gewöhnlicher Mensch, ein Zauberer, ein böses Vorzeichen, ein Unruhstifter, ein (schreckhafte) Visionen erzeugender Gaukler."*

5. Cf. Rémi Siméon: *Dictionnaire de la langue nahuatl ou mexicaine* (Paris: Imprimerie Nationale, 1885); and Andrés de Olmos: *Grammaire de la langue nahuatl ou mexicaine* (Paris: Imprimerie Nationale, 1875), p. 229. *"Von ihm wird gesagt: er wirft auf die Leute die Türkisschlange, den Feuerbohrer, d. h. den Krieg"* (Seler, *loc. cit.*). Cf. also Bernardino de Sahagún, *Historia general de las cosas de Nueva España* (Mexico: Pedro Robredo, 1938), Vol. IV, pp. 101–102, *". . . nuestro dios Vitzilopuchtli usaba de dos cosas para contra sus enemigos para aterrarlos y ahuyentarlos; la una se llama* xiucóatl, *y la otra* mamalhoaztli *. . . . y él tenía por cetro real en la mano una culebra hecha de mosaico, que llaman* xiucóatl, *no derecha sino tortuosa o combada, y aquella, siendo vivo, como nigromántico en las batallas como gran serpiente viva la echaba sobre los enemigos con que los espantaba y hacía huir."* Cf. also Bernardino de Sahagún, *Historia general de las cosas de Nueva España* (Ángel María Garibay K., ed.; Editorial Porrúa, S. A., 1956; hereafter referred to as Sahagún, Garibay ed.), Vol. IV, p. 159.

6. In Bernardino de Sahagún: *Historia de las cosas de Nueva España* (Francisco del Paso y Troncoso, ed.; Madrid: Hauser y Menet, 1906, Vol. VII; hereafter referred to as *Real Palacio MS*) the text reads: *ylhuiq'xtililoya.*

7. The meaning (*cf. tealtia*) is to offer as a sacrifice, or to bathe or anoint (*cf.* Sahagún, Garibay ed. Vol. III, pp. 43, 56).

And he was thus arrayed: he had an ear pendant of lovely cotinga feathers;[8] his disguise was the fire serpent. He had the blue netted sash,[9] he had the maniple.[10] He wore bells, he wore shells.[11]

Auh ynjc muchichioaia: xiuhtotonacoche catca, xiuhcoanaoale, xiuhtlalpile, matacaxe, tzitzile, oiuoalle.

---

8. *Xiuhtototl: Cotinga amabilis* Gould. Herbert Friedmann, Ludlow Griscom, and Robert T. Moore: "Distributional Check-List of the Birds of Mexico," *Pacific Coast Avifauna*, Nos. 29 & 33 (Berkeley, Calif.: Cooper Ornithological Club, 1950, 1957; henceforth referred to as Friedmann *et al.*). Pt. II, p. 59.

9. *Xiuhtlalpile*: The *Primeros Memoriales MS* reads: *Xiuhtlalpilli inic motzinilpiticac*, suggesting it was worn about the hips. See *Primeros Memoriales* in Francisco del Paso y Troncoso, ed.: *Historia general de las cosas de Nueva España por Fray Bernardino de Sahagún: edición parcial en facsímile de los Códices Matritenses en lengua mexicana* (Madrid: Hauser y Menet, 1905), Vol. VI.

10. *Matacaxtli: "Ajorca, pulsera. Un adorno de tela que se colocaba sobre el antebrazo, y en la muñeca precisamente, y caía a un lado y a otro, a manera de los manípulos del rito romano."* Sahagún, (Garibay ed.), Vol. IV, p. 341.

11. The *Primeros Memoriales MS* reads: *tzitzilli, oyoalli in icxic.* Garibay thus phrases the passage: *"Hay sonajillas y cascabeles en sus piernas."* Sahagún (Garibay ed.), Vol. IV, p. 279.

Second Chapter, which telleth of the god named Paynal (He who Hasteneth), whom they worshipped and to whom they offered sacrifices in ancient times.

Paynal was "the delegate," "the substitute," "the deputy," because he represented Uitzilopochtli. When there was a procession he was given the name Paynal, because[12] they pressed him on quickly; he was made to hasten.[13]

And the people followed him; they followed him in pursuit. They went howling,[14] crying war cries. They went raising the dust, making the ground smoke. Like a thing possessed, the earth rumbled.

And one man went carrying [the image] in his arms.

And he was thus arrayed: he went garbed in the costly cape of precious feathers.[15] The quetzal feather device went placed on him.[16] He had bars painted upon his face;[17] he had the star design painted upon his face. His face was painted with the star design.[18] He had a turquoise nose rod. His was the hummingbird disguise. He had the breast mirror; he had a shield set with a mosaic of turquoise.

Jnic vme capitulo, ytechpa tlatoa yn teutl yn jtoca paynal: yn qujmoteutiaia, yoan in qujtlamanjliaia ie uecauh.

Paynal: motepatillotianj, moteixiptlatianj: tepan mixeoanj: iehica ca qujmixiptlatiaia, in vitzilubuchtli, yn iquac tlaiaoaloaia, motocaiotia paynal: ipampa ca cenca, qujtototzaia, qujmotlalochtiaia.

Auh in maceoalti, qujtocaia, qujtlalochtocaia, coiohujtiuja, quicaoatztiuja, teuhtli quiquetztiuja, tlalli qujpototztiuja: iuhqujn tlaixqujqujça, tlalli tetecujca:

auh ce tlacatl qujnapalotiuja.

Auh ynjc muchichioaia, teuquemetiuja, quetzalapanecaiutl, in contlalitiuja, ixoacalichioale, ixcitlalichioale, mixcitlalichiuh, xiuhiacamjoa, vitzitzilnaoale, eltezcaoa, xiuhchimale.

---

12. The *Real Palacio MS* adds *q'paynaltiaya* — they make him run with agility.

13. Sahagún (*Florentine Codex,* corresponding Spanish text) describes Paynal as *ligero, apressurado.*

14. The suffix *"tiuja"* is consistently written *"tiviya"* in *Real Palacio MS.*

15. Seler (*Gesammelte Abhandlungen,* Vol. II, p. 431) defines it as a costly robe made entirely of precious feathers, worn over the *xicolli* (jacket) and the *tzitzicaztilmatli* (cape worn over the jacket); probably it was an apron-like garment placed on the front of the idols.

16. *Apanecaiutl: "'Adorno en forma de travesaño.' Insignia de honor y ornato, consistente en una banda de plumas que atraviesa de hombro a costado."* Sahagún, (Garibay ed.) Vol. IV, p. 321.

17. *Ixoacalchioale*: literally: "face design like a wooden carrying frame."

18. *Real Palacio MS.: mizçitlalichiuh.*

Third Chapter, which telleth of the god named Tezcatlipoca (Smoking Mirror), whom they worshipped and to whom they offered sacrifices in ancient times.

Jnic ey, capitulo, ytechpa tlatoa in teutl, yn jtoca tezcatlipoca: in qujmoteutiaia, yoan in qujtlamanjliaia, ie uecauh.

Tezcatlipoca: he was considered a true god, whose abode was everywhere — in the land of the dead, on earth, [and] in heaven. When he walked on the earth, he quickened vice and sin. He introduced anguish and affliction.

Tezcatlipoca: ynin vel teutl ipan machoia, noujian ynemjian: mictla, tlalticpac, ylhujcac. Jn jquac nemja tlalticpac, iehoatl qujiolitiaja, in teuhtli tlaçolli: cococ teupouhquj, qujteittitiaia,

He brought discord among people, wherefore he was called "the enemy on both sides." He created, he brought down all things. He cast his shadow on one, he visited one with all the evils which befall men; he mocked, he ridiculed men.

tetzalã, tenepantla motecaia: ipampa y, mjtoaia necoc iautl, muchi qujiocoiaia, qujtemoujaja, qujteecaujltiaia, qujtecujtiaia, yn jxquich aqualli tepan muchioaia: teca maujltiaia, tequequeloaia.

But sometimes he bestowed riches — wealth, heroism, valor, position of dignity,[19] rulership, nobility, honor.[20]

Auh in quenman, qujtemacaia, in necujltonolli: in tlatqujtl, in oqujchiotl, in tiacauhiutl, in tecuiotl, in tlatocaiutl, in pillotl, in mauizçotl.

19. *Yn tiyacauhyotl yn teucyotl* in *ibid.*

20. *Ym mavizyotl* in *ibid.*

Fourth Chapter, which telleth of the god named Tlaloc, the provider.[21]

Tlaloc, the provider. To him was attributed the rain; for he created, brought down, showered down the rain and the hail. He caused the trees, the grasses, the maize to blossom, to sprout, to leaf out, to bloom, to grow. And also were attributed to him the drowning of people, the thunderbolts.

And he was thus arrayed:[22] his face was covered with soot; his face was painted with liquid rubber; it was anointed with black; his face was [spotted] with [a paste of] amaranth seed dough.[23] He had a sleeveless cloud-jacket of netted fabric; he had a sleeveless dew-jacket of netted fabric; he had a crown of heron feathers; he had a necklace of green stone jewels. He had foam sandals,[24] and also bells. He had a green and white plaited reed banner.[25]

Jnjc nauj capitulo, ytechpa tlatoaia yn teutl, yn jtoca tlaloc, tlamacazquj.

Tlaloc, tlamacazquj: ynjn ipan machoia, in qujiaujtl: ca iehoatl quiiocoaia, qujtemoujaia, qujpixoaia, in quijaujtl, yoan in teciujtl: quixotlaltiaja, qujtzmolinaltiaja, qujxoxuvialtiaja, quicueponaltiaja, quizcaltiaia in quaujtl, in çacatl, in tonacaiotl. Yoan no itech tlamjloia, in teilaqujliztli, in tlaujtequjliztli.

Auh ynjc muchichioaia, tlaixtlilpopotzalli, tlaixolhujlli, motliloçac, ixmjchioave, ixmichioauhio, auachxicole, aiauhxicole, aztatzone, chalchiuhcozque, poçulcaque, no tzitzile, aztapilpane.

21. *Tlamacazqui*: *"lit.,* el que dará algo. *De donde dos sentidos: a) El que dará lo necesario para la vida; o sea, el Proveedor divino. En este primer sentido se aplica a los dioses, en especial a los de la lluvia. b) El que dará algo para el servicio de los dioses, y en este sentido se aplica a los ministros secundarios del culto de los antiguos mexicanos."* Garibay, *Hist. de la Lit. Náhuatl,* Vol. II, p. 408.

22. *Auh yvin ymmochichivaya* in *Real Palacio MS.*

23. Cf. Sahagún (Garibay Ed.), Vol. I, p. 200; see also Seler, *op. cit.,* Vol. II, pp. 443–4. The *Primeros Memoriales MS* gives *yyoztopil, "su baston de junco."* Cf. Miguel León-Portilla: *Ritos, Sacerdotes y Atavíos de los Dioses,* Fuentes Indígenas de la Cultura Náhuatl, Textos de los Informantes de Sahagún, 1 (Mexico: Universidad Nacional Autónoma de México, Instituto de Historia, Seminario de Cultura Náhuatl, 1958), p. 121.

24. *Poçolcaque*: *"de algodón flojo y blando,"* Sahagún, *op. cit.,* Vol. IV, p. 281.

25. Cf. Sahagún, *op. cit.,* Vol. I, p. 162.

Fifth Chapter, which telleth of the god named Quetzalcoatl (Plumed Serpent).

Quetzalcoatl — he was the wind; he was the guide, the roadsweeper of the rain gods,[26] of the masters of the water, of those who brought rain. And when the wind increased, it was said, the dust swirled up, it roared, howled, became dark, blew in all directions; there was lightning; it grew wrathful.

And he was thus arrayed: he had a conical ocelot skin cape. His face was covered with soot. He was adorned with [spiral] wind and mesquite symbols.[27] He had a curved, [turquoise mosaic] ear pendant.[28] He wore a gold neckband of small seashells.[29] He bore the precious pheasant device on his back.[30] He had ocelot skin anklets with bells. He wore a cotton bone [ribbed] jacket.[31] His were the shield with the wind-shell design,[32] the curved [inlaid] spear-thrower,[33] and also the foam sandals.

Jnic macujlli capitulo, ytechpa tlatoa yn teutl, yn jtoca quetzalcoatl.

Quetzalcoatl: yn ehecatl ynteiacancauh yntlachpancauh in tlaloque, yn aoaque, yn qujqujiauhti. Auh yn jquac molhuja eheca, mjtoa: teuhtli quaqualaca, ycoioca, tetecujca, tlatlaiooa, tlatlalpitza, tlatlatzinj, motlatlaueltia.

Auh yujn yn muchichioaia: ocelocopile, mjxtlilpopotz, hecanechioale, mizqujnechioale, tzicoliuhcanacoche, teucujtlaacuechcozque, quetzalcoxollamamale, ocelotzitzile, icpaomjcicujle, hecacozcachimale, hecaujque, no poçulcaque.

26. Cf. Eduard Seler: *Tonalamatl of the Aubin Collection* (London and Aylesbury: Hazell, Watson and Viney, Ltd., 1901), pp. 42–43; and Juan de Torquemada: *Segunda parte de los veinte i un libros rituales i monarchia indiana* (Madrid: Nicholas Rodriguez Franco, 1723), pp. 47 and 52. The connection between Quetzalcoatl and the Tlalocs is illustrated in a passage in Sahagún, *op. cit.*, Vol. II, p. 263: *"Esta gente atribuia el viento a un dios que llamaban* Quetzalcóatl, *bien casi como dios de los vientos. Sopla el viento de cuatro partes del mundo por mandamiento de este dios, según ellos decían; de la una parte viene de hacia el oriente donde ellos dicen estar el paraíso terrenal al cual llaman* Tlalocan, *(y) a este viento le llamaban* tlalocáyotl; *no es viento furioso, cuando él sopla no impide (a) las canoas andar por el agua."*

27. Wind-painting, according to Seler, *Gesammelte Abhandlungen,* Vol, II, p. 435; see also pp. 436 and 437.

28. In corresponding Spanish text, Sahagún, writing more fully than in the Aztec text, says: *"Tenja, vnas orejeras, de turquesas, de labor mosayco. . . ."*

29. The corresponding Spanish text of Sahagún reads: *"tenja vn collar de oro, de que colgauan, vnos caracolitos mariscos, preciosos."*

30. Cf. Garibay, *op. cit.*, Vol. I, p. 379.

31. See Eduard Seler, *op. cit.*, p. 435.

32. Sahagún's corresponding Spanish text has: *"vna rodela, con vna pintura, con cinco angulos: que llaman, el joel de viento."* The term *ecacozcachimalli* may be translated more literally as "shield with pendant shell" design. A bisected shell design usually hangs as a breast shield on representations of Quetzalcoatl; this same design appears on the shield. (See *Tonalamatl of Codex Borbonicus.*)

33. Corresponding Spanish text says: *"era como empuñadora de espada."*

Sixth Chapter: here are named the highest of the goddesses whom the natives worshipped, whom they falsely revered as divine.

Ciuacoatl (Snake-woman) [was called][34] a savage beast and an evil omen.[35] She was an evil omen to men; she brought men misery. For, it was said, she gave men the digging stick, the tump-line; she visited men therewith.

And as she appeared before men, she was covered with chalk, like a court lady. She wore ear plugs, obsidian ear plugs. She appeared in white, garbed in white, standing white, pure white. Her womanly hairdress rose up.[36]

By night she walked weeping, wailing; also was she an omen of war.[37]

And in this wise was her image arrayed: her face was painted one-half red, one-half black.[38] She had a headdress of [eagle] feathers;[39] she had golden ear plugs. She wore a triangular shoulder shawl. She carried a turquoise [mosaic] weaving-stick.

Jnjc chiquacẽ capitulo: vncan moteneoa, yn oc cenca tlapanauja yn cioateteu: yn qujnmoteutiaia, in qujnteutlapiqujaia yn njcan tlaca.

Cioacoatl tequanj: yoan tetzaujtl, tetetzaujanj, icnoiutl qujteittitia: ca mjtoaia, victli mecapalli, qujtemacaia, ic temotlaia.

Auh ynjc moteittitiaia, motenextiliaia: iuhqujn tecpan cioatl, nanacoche, iitznacoche, iztaian moquetza, iztaian actica, iztacatla ycaia, iztazticac, vel panj qujquetza yn jneaxtlaoal, yn jaxtlacujl,

ioaltica chocatinenca, tecoiouhtinenca, no iautetzaujtl catca.

Auh yuj yn muchichioaia yxiptla, yn jxaiac, centlacochichiltic, centlacotliltic, yujquatzone, teucujtlanacoche, quechqueme, xiuhtzotzopace.

34. The *Real Palacio* MS adds *mitoaya.*

35. Cf. also *tetzauhcoatl,* species of snake mentioned by Sahagún (Garibay ed.), Vol. III, p. 271.

36. *Quiqueq[ue]tza* in *Real Palacio MS.*

37. This is explained in Sahagún (Garibay ed.), Vol. II, pp. 284, 287.

38. See illustration, which indicates that the part of the face below the nose is black.

39. *Yquauhtzon* in *Primeros Memoriales. "Su corona de plumas de águila"* in Sahagún, *op. cit.*, Vol. IV, p. 285.

Seventh Chapter: here is named the goddess called Chicome coatl (Seven Snake).[40]

Chicome coatl: this one represented — she was the representative of — maize and men's sustenance of whatever sort; what is drunk, what is eaten.

And thus was her array: her face was painted with red ochre; she had a paper headdress; she wore a shift [ornamented with] water flowers and a skirt [ornamented with] water flowers; also she had foam sandals; she carried the shield with the sun sign, the sun shield.

Jnic chicome capitulo: vncan moteneoa, yn cioateutl: yn jtoca, chicome coatl.

Chicome coatl: iehoatl ipan mjxeoaia, qujmjxiptlatiaia, in tonacaiotl: yoan in çaço tlein ynenca, yiolca maceoalli, yn joa, yn qualo.

Auh yujn yn nechichioale catca; ixtlauhxaoale, amacale, axochiavipile, axochiacueie, no poçulcaque, tonalchimale, tonatiuhchimale.

40. See Pl. 29, which explains the name.

Eighth Chapter: here is named the goddess called Teteo innan (Mother of the Gods), who is also named Tlalli yiollo (Heart of the Earth) and Toci (Our Grandmother).

Jnic chicuei, capitulo: vncã moteneoa, yn cioateutl, yn jtoca: Teteu ynna: no motocaiotia, Tlalli yiollo, yoan Toçi.

She was the mother of the gods. The physicians, the leeches, those who cured hemorrhoids, those who purged people, those who cured eye ailments worshipped her.

Jnnã catca yn teteu, qujmoteutiaja, in titici, in teitzmjnque, tetzinanque, tetlanoqujlique, teixpatique.

Also women, midwives, those who administered sedatives at childbirth, those who brought about abortions, who read the future, who cast auguries by looking upon water or by casting grains of maize, who read fortunes by use of knotted cords, who removed [intrusive] objects from the body, who removed worms from the teeth, who removed worms from the eyes.[41]

Auh yn cioa, temjxiujtique, tepillalilique, tetlatlaxilique, tlapouhque, atlan teittanj, tlaolchaiauhque, mecatlapouhque, tetlacujcujlique, tetlanocujlanque, teixocujlanque.

Likewise owners of sweat-houses prayed to her; wherefore they caused her image to be placed in the front of the sweat-house. They called her "Grandmother of the Baths."

No iehoantin qujtlatlauhtiaia, in temazcaleque; ypampa y, quitlaliliaia yn jxiptla, in temazcalixquac, qujtocaiotiaia, temazcalteci.

And when a feast day was celebrated for her, when it was the time of the slaying of the one who was the impersonator of Teteo innan, the physicians sought to banish her sorrow, that she might not weep. They amused her, they flattered her, they satisfied her caprices, they made her happy. They wished her not to weep.[42] They hid [her fate] from her,[43] they made merry with one another about death. They skirmished, they made war, they cried war-cries, battle-cries, for her. Devices were exhibited, there was giving of devices, there was giving of gifts which became the binding force of the valiant warriors, wherefore they painted them with white chalk, wherefore they pasted them with downy feathers. They surrounded her so that they stood over her.

Auh yn jquac, in ie ilhujqujxtililoia, in ie imjquiztequippa: in iehoantin titici, yn jxiptla catca teteu ynna, qujtlaoculpopoloaia, amo vel chocaia, queelelqujxtiaia, qujtlanenectiaia, qujtlanenequjltiaia, qujceceltiaia, haqujchoctlanja, qujtlatlahtitiaia, momjquizquequeloaia, qujnecaliltiaia, qujiaochioaia, qujtlacaoachiliaia, coiuujaia, tlauiznextiloia, netlauizmacoia, netlauhtiloia: in qujmjliuhca muchioaia in tiiacaoa, ic quintiçaujaia, ic qujnpotonjaia, qujmotzacujlitiuja, ic panj moquetzaia.

41. Sahagún describes these words in detail. See Ángel María Garibay K.: *"Paralipómenos de Sahagún,"* in *Tlalocan,* Vol. II, No. 3 (1947), pp. 235–54.

42. *Ha' quichoctlama* in *Real Palacio MS.*

43. Cf. also Sahagún (Garibay ed.), Vol. I, pp. 122, 191.

And when she who was the likeness [of the goddess] was slain, then a man put on her skin and stood between two of his Huaxtecs,[44] who accompanied him on either side.

They were painted with white chalk and with [marks like] hawk scratches. They went naked, with a rope for a breech-clout. On their backs they carried a paper crown provided with protruding spindles, cotton flowers, and quetzal feathers.[45]

They brought to Tocititlan [the man wearing the skin of the victim]; they left her skin upon a wooden bench.[46]

And the array [of Teteo innan] was as follows: there was liquid rubber on her lips; [the representation of] a hole was placed on each cheek. She had cotton flowers. She had a ball with palm strips.[47] She had a shell-covered skirt, called a star-skirt. She had the star-skirt. Eagle feathers were strewn over her shift — it was strewn with eagle [feathers]; it had white eagle feathers, pointed eagle feathers. Her golden shield was perforated in the center. She carried a bird foot. She used a broom; she carried a broom.

Auh yn jquac onmjc, yn jxiptla: njman ce tlacatl onmaqujaia, yn jeoaio, ynnepantla oalmoquetzaia, vmentin ycuexoa, qujujcaia, qujtzatzacutiujia:

motiçauique, motlotloujtecque, çan pepetlauhtiuj, in memecamaxtli: amacalli in qujmama, mahmalacaquetzallo, ichcaxochiio, hiujquetzallo:

vmpa concaoa, in tocititlan: quauhtlapechco contlaliaia yn jeoaio.

Auh ynjc nechichioale, motenolcopi, tlaxapuchtli qujmotlatlalili yn jcamapã ichcaxochioa, çoiatemale, cuechcueie, mocuechcueti: ic mjtoa, citlalli ycue, citlalcueie, quavîvih, tzetzeliuhquj yn juipil, quauhtzetzeliuhquj, iztac quavihujio, quauhteuitzço; yn jchimal, teucujtlaytixapo, totoicxiio, popoa, izqujce.

44. Seler, *Einige Kapitel,* p. 6. Cf. also Sahagún, *op. cit.,* p. 193, referring to the Toçi festival: "*iban delante de ellos aquellos sus devotos que se llaman* icuexóan."

45. See Pl. 8.

46. Sahagún, *ibid.,* p. 196, calls it *garita.*

47. Garibay translates *yçoiatemal* as "*su mechón, de palma.*" Sahagún (Garibay ed.), Vol. IV, p. 283.

Ninth Chapter: here is named the goddess called Tzapotlan tenan (the Mother of Tzapotlan).

She was represented as a woman. From her substance was made turpentine.

She healed the bodies of men, those with itch of the head.[48] Those who were hoarse used the turpentine unguent on the throat; [they used it] who had sores or pimples on the head,[49] or cracks in the skin of the feet, the lips, the face, the hands, the legs; and for jigger fleas, for the tortilla-sickness.[50] Its oil, its heat were required on indeed many occasions.[51]

And when the feast day was celebrated,[52] they who sold the turpentine unguent bought slaves and slew them. They fashioned her image of amaranth seed dough. Her old men sang for her; they beat the two-toned drum; they beat, they struck the turtle-shell drum; they rattled the gourd rattle; they rasped the notched bone for her.

The array [of Tzapotlan tenan] was as follows: two [drops] were painted on her face; she had a paper crown; large drops of liquid rubber and small drops were spattered over her paper crown, and it had quetzal feathers arranged to resemble corn-tassels. She carried the mist rattle-board.[53]

Jnjc chicunauj, capitulo: vncan moteneoa yn cioateutl, yn jtoca Tzaputla tena.

Ce cioatl, ipan mjxeoaia, yn oxitl ynacaio muchioaia:

quipaleuja yn tenacaio, yn aqujn quaxocociuj, tozcamjiaoaciuj, motozcaoxiuja: chaquachiuj, quaçaoati, xotzaianj, tentzaianj, ixteteçonauj, mateteçonauj, icxitzatzaianj, yoan in qualo, yn tlaxcaliciuj: yn jchiaoaca yn jtonal vel mieccan monequj.

Auh yn jquac ilhujquixtiloia, yn oxinamacaque, motlacacoujaia, tlacamjctiaia, qujtzooallotiaia yn jxiptla, qujcujcatiaia, yn iveveiooan, qujteponacilhujaia, caiotzotzonjlia, caioujtequjlia, caiacachilhuja, comjchicaoacilhuja.

Jnjc nechichioale omexaoale, amacale, olchachapanquj, tlaolchipinilli yn jamacal, yoan quetzalmjiaoaio, aiuchicaoace.

---

48. "*... vna manera, de bubas, o sarna: que nace, en la cabeça*" (corresponding Spanish text).

49. "*... otra enfermedad ... assi mjsmo, que nace en la cabeça: que es como bubas*" (*loc. cit.*).

50. The *Real Palacio MS* reads: "*yoan in cualo yn tlaxcalicivi.*" Seler (*op. cit.*, p. 7) translates: "*und wenn gegessen wird, an der Maisfladenkrankheit leiden.*" A nearly identical passage in the Appendix of Book I reads: "*yoan in qualocatl, intech motlalia, in tlaxcaliciuiztli.*" This rendition seems preferable and is followed in our translation. A passage in Sahagún (*op. cit.*, Vol. III, p. 177) may clarify: "*... algunos curan esto con la penca del maguey cortando un pedazo a manera de parche, y poniéndola en el nacido, y abriéndola por medio para que quede descubierta la boca del nacido, y tomar un poco de* óxitl *y ponerlo en la propia boca del nacido, de suerte que poniendo fuego sobre el* óxitl *quede quemado el nacido.... su comida del enfermo serán tortillas tostadas....*"

51. This phrase might also be rendered: "When corpulence was one's lot, it was required in indeed many places."

52. *Ylhuiq'xtililoya* in *Real Palacio MS.*

53. *Aiuchicaoace:* "*'Sonajero de niebla.' Tabla con sonajas intercaladas que resonaban al andar el que la llevaba en hombros*" (Sahagún, *op. cit.*, Vol. IV, p. 324). Ángel María Garibay K., in *Veinte Himnos Sacros de los Nahuas*, Fuentes Indígenas de la Cultura Náhuatl, Informantes de Sahagún, 2 (Mexico: Universidad Nacional Autónoma de México, Instituto de Historia: Seminario de Cultura Náhuatl, 1958), p. 59, states: "*En la relación de la fiesta del Etzalcualiztli se describe ampliamente el instrumento que, en sentido mágico era el procurador de la lluvia. Una tabla con huecos, en los cuales se colocaba el sonajero, o sea una serie de sonajas que al andar quien portaba este instrumento sonaban raramente. Era como la emulación de los truenos de Tláloc, que hace sonar sus vasijas cuando el rayo estalla.*" Cf. Seler: *Gesammelte Abhandlungen*, Vol. II, pp. 474, 989.

Tenth Chapter, which telleth of the goddesses [called] Ciuapipiltin.[54]

These were five devils, whose images were of stone.[55] Of them it was supposed and men said: "They hate people; they mock them." When one was under their spell, possessed, one's mouth was twisted, one's face was contorted; one lacked use of a hand; one's feet were misshapen — one's feet were deadened; one's hand trembled; one foamed at the mouth. Whence it was said, one had met and contended with the Ciuapipiltin, who dwelt at the crossroads. Wherefore fathers or mothers told their children: "Go not forth; the Ciuapipiltin arrive on earth; they descend."

And for this reason, when it was their feast day, they made them offerings of soft, folded tortillas, butterfly-shaped tortillas, S-shaped tortillas,[56] small tamales,[57] toasted grains of maize.

And then they offered all these, sometimes at the temple of the goddesses, sometimes at the crossroads.

And their array was [thus]: They had their faces whitened with chalk, and, over this, anointed with liquid rubber. Their paper garments were covered over with the obsidian point design.[58] They had sandals decked with feathers.

Jnic matlactli, capitulo: yntechpa tlatoa, yn cioateteu, cioapipilti:

Diablome catca y, macujltin, teme yn jmixiptlaoan; intech tlamjloia, qujlmach tetlauelia, teca mocaiaoa, ynjc aca itech qujneoaia, tlauelilocati, tennecujliuj, ixnecujliuj, matzicoliuj, icxicopichauj, icximjmjquj, momacuecuetza, tenqualacquiça: ic mjtoaia omotenamicti, ypan oquizque cioapipilti, vmaxac chaneque. Jpampa y yn tetaoa, anoço tenaoa, qujmilhujaia yn jnpilhoan; maca xonqujça, tlalpan aci, temo in cioapipilti.

Auh ipampa y, yn iquac ymjlhujuh, ynjc qujntlamanjliaia: tlamatzoalli, papalotlaxcalli, xonecujli, xocuichtlamatzoalli, izqujtl.

Auh yn vncan momana y, in quenman vncan yn cioateucalco, in quenman, vmaxac.

Auh yn jnnechichioal catca, mjxtiçauique: auh panj tlaolxaoalti, tlaitzcopeoaltectli, tlaitzcopeoalli, yn jmamatlaquen, potoncacaqueque.

54. Cf. Seler, *op. cit.*, Vol. II, p. 498.

55. The *Real Palacio MS* adds *catca*.

56. *Xonecujli:* "'*pie torcido.' Pan en forma de zigzag, usado en ciertas fiestas*" (Sahagún, *op. cit.*, p. 370).

57. *Xocuichtlamatzoalli: "Tamales de fruta y bledos" (loc. cit.).*

58. After *tlaitzcopeoaltectli* the *Real Palacio MS* adds *yn imamatlaquē*.

Eleventh Chapter, which telleth of the goddess named Chalchiuhtli ycue (the Jade-skirted), who was [goddess of] the waters.

She was considered a god[dess]. They represented her as a woman.[59] So it was claimed, it was said that she belonged to the rain-gods, as their elder sister.

Hence she was esteemed, feared, held in awe; hence she caused terror. She drowned one, plunged one in water, submerged one; she caused the water to foam, to billow over one; she caused the water to swirl over one. Thereby she carried one into the depths.

She upset the boat, overturned it, lifted it up, tossed it up, plunged it in the water.

And sometimes she sank one, drowned one. The water was restless; the waves roared; they dashed and resounded. The water was wild.

When it calmed, when it quieted, it heaved to and fro; it was said, "It playeth, it swelleth, it splasheth; the water striketh the shore, spraying water and foaming."

And when there was no wind, it was calm; the water spread like a mirror, gleaming, glittering.

And when her feast day was celebrated,[60] it was likewise in [the month of] Etzalqualiztli,[61] when the feast day of the rain-gods was celebrated.

They formed her image over a framework of wood; they put a skirt upon her, and a shift; they placed a necklace upon her — a plaited necklace, from which hung a golden disc.

And they offered her offerings; her fire priests came out to receive her. They strewed the *yiauhtli* herb before her.

Jnic matlactli vce capitulo: ytechpa tlatoa, yn cioateutl, yn jtoca chalchiuhtli ycue: iehoatl yn atl.

Teutl ipan machoia: iuhqujn cioatl qujxiptlatiaia, iuh mjtoaia, qujlmach ynvan pouj, inueltiuh in tlaloque:

ynic mauiztililoia, ynic imacaxoia, ynjc mauhcaittoia, ynjc tlamauhtiaia, teatoctiaia, teatlanmjctiaia, tepolactiaia, tepan poçonja, moteponaçoa, maxiciotia, tepan moteujlacachoa, ynjc tecentlanjujca:

yn acalli qujcuepa, qujxtlapachcuepa, queoatiquetza, ca aco maiauj, ca tema.

Auh in quenma teapachoa, teapotzauja, mocueiotia, titicujca, xaxamacatimanj, cocomocatimanj, hatlacamanj:

yn jquac oceuh, yn ie ceuj, aujc iaiauh: qujtoa, maujltia, xixiqujpiliuj, cocomotzauj, atentli itech onmotlatlatzoa, onmochachaquanja, mapopoçoquillotia.

Auh yn jquac atle ehecatl, tlamattimanj, atezcattimanj, petlantimanj, cuecueiocatimanj.

Auh yn jquac ilhuiqujxtiloia, çan no iquac yn etzalqualiztli: yn vncan ilhujqujxtililoia tlaloque,

colotli in qujchichioaia yxiptla: qujcuetiaia, qujujpiltiaia, qujcozcatiaia, cozcapetlatl, itech pilcatiuh cuztic teucujtlacomalli:

yoan qujtlamanjliaia, qujnanamiquj yn jtlenamacacauh, yiauhtli, ixpan qujtepevilia,

59. *Quixiptlayotiaya* in *Real Palacio MS.*

60. *Ylhuiq'xtililoya* in *Real Palacio MS.*

61. Sahagún (Garibay ed., Vol. I, p. 166): *"este* etzalli *era hecho de maíz cocido, a manera de arroz, y era muy amarillo."* Diego de Durán: *Historia de las Indias de Nueva España y islas de Tierra Firme* (Mexico: J. M. Andrade y F. Escalante, 1867–1880), Vol. II, p. 210: *"el maiz cocido por si solo llamanle pozolly pero a causa de revolverlo con frijol* (etl) *le llaman etzally."*

With the mist rattle-board they went speaking; the elders of the *calpulli*, her singers, sang for her.

caiochicaoaz ilhujtinemj, qujcujcatia in calpoleque, ycujcacaoan.

And right before her image died a woman slave whom they had bought. The water merchants exhibited her; those who gained their livelihoods from water, those who brought water in boats, those who owned boats, those who lived on the water, the boatmakers, those who served water in the market place.[62]

Auh in vel ixiptla, yquac mjquja: tlacotli cioatl in qujcoaia, iehoan qujnextiaia, yn anamacaque: yn atl yc motlaiecultia, yn acaltica atlacuj, yn acaleque, yn apantlaca: yoan acalquetzque tianquizco, in qujtechieltia atl.

Likewise they arrayed her, made offerings, and ornamented her; for she would go, when she died, to a place called Tlalocan. In the temple of the Tlalocs they opened her breast.

No iuh qujchichioaia, no iuh qujtlamamacaia, no iuh qujcencaoaia: iuh tlantiuja: in miquja, ytocaiocan tlalocan: yn vncan inteupan, tlaloque, queltetequja.

Then Moctezuma especially honored [the goddess]. Before her image incense was offered;[63] he beheaded quail for her.

Jn jquac y, no cenca qujmauiztiliaia, yn motecuçuma: ixpan tlenamacoia yn jxiptla, qujtlacotonjlia,

Thus they said: "The lord gaineth rain; he doth a penance for his people." And then they were thankful as they paid honor to the waters, [for] they remembered that because of her we live. She is our sustenance. And thence come all things that are necessary.

iuh qujtoaia: qujiauhtlatlanj in tlacatl, qujtlamacehuja yn jmaceoal: yoan vncan mocnelilmati, ynjc qujmahujztiliaia atl: qujlnamjquja, ca ic tinemj, ca tonenca: yoan ic muchioa, yn ixqujch tetech monequj.

Also in the same manner they honored the image of the maize, named Chicome coatl; and the image of the salt, named Uixtociuatl. Thus they remembered the three.[64] For they become indeed the livelihood of the people; through them the people are satisfied; through them they can live.

No iuh qujmauiztiliaia, yn jxiptla tonacaiotl, yn jtoca, chicome coatl; yoã yn jxiptla iztatl, ytoca Vixtocioatl: ic qujlnamjquja; yn je tlamanjxti: ca vel ynenca muchioa in maceoalli, ic vellamati, ic vel nemj.

And she was thus arrayed: her face was painted; she was painted about the lips with blue, her lips were painted blue; her face was painted yellow.[65] She had a green-stone necklace; she had turquoise [mosaic] ear plugs. She had a blue paper crown with a spray of quetzal feathers. Her shift, her skirt were painted like water waves. She bore a shield ornamented with a water lily. She carried the mist rattle-board,[66] which she sounded. She wore foam sandals.

Auh yujn, in muchichioaia: moxaoaia, texotica, motenujltec, motexotenujltec, mjxcoçalhuj, chalchiuhcuzque, xiuhnacoche, texoamacale, quetzalmjiaoaio, atlacujlolhvipile, atlacujlolhuiujpile, atlacujlolcueie, atlacueçonanchimale, aiuchicaoaçe, cacalaca; poçulcaque.

---

62. Corresponding Spanish text of the *Florentine Codex* reads: "*. . . la festejauan . . . todos aquellos, que tienẽ sus granjerias, en el agua: como son los que venden agua, en canoas: y los que venden agua, en tinajas, en la plaça. . . .*"

63. *Tlenamacaya* in *Real Palacio MS.*

64. Corresponding Spanish text: "*. . . porque dezian, que estas tres diosas: mantenjan, a la gente popular: para que pudiessen, viujr, y multiplicar.*"

65. Corresponding Spanish text: "*. . . la pintauan, la cara, con color amarilla. . . .*"

66. Corresponding Spanish text: "*Tenja en la mano, derecha, vn vaso, con vna cruz: hecho a manera, de la custodia, en que se lleua el sacramento, quando vno solo le lleua: y era como cetro, desta diosa.*" See illustrations of Chalchiuhtli ycue and Tzapotlan tenan.

Twelfth Chapter, which telleth of Tlaçolteotl.

Tlaçolteotl, also called Ixcuina, was besides called Tlaelquani. As to her being named Tlaçolteotl: it was said that it was because her realm, her domain, was that of evil and perverseness — that is to say, lustful and debauched living. It was said that she ruled and was mistress of lust and debauchery.[67]

And as to her name Ixcuina: it was said there were four women — the first named Tiacapan (the first born), the second Teicu (the younger sister), the third named Tlaco (the middle sister), the fourth named Xocotzin (the youngest sister).[68] These four women, it was said, were god[desses]. Each one of these was called Tlaçolteotl.

And as for her being called Tlaelquani:[69] it was said it was because one told, one recited before her, all vanities; one told, one spread before her all unclean works — however ugly, however grave; avoiding nothing because of shame. Indeed all was exposed, told before her.

The confession[70]

It was said: evil and perverseness, debauched living — these Tlaçolteotl offered one, cast upon one, inspired in one. And likewise she forgave, set aside, removed [corruption]. She cleansed one; she washed one. In her hand lay the blue and yellow waters.[71]

Jnic matlactli vmome capitulo: ytechpa tlatoa yn tlaçolteutl.

In tlaçulteutl: yoan itoca ixcujna, yoan itoca tlaelquanj. Jnic motocaiotia tlaçulteutl, qujl ipampa, qujl iehoatl yiaxca, ytlatquj, ytech pouj, in teuhtli, in tlaçulli: in qujtoznequj, avilnemjliztli, qujl ipan tecuti, ypan tlatocati, yn aujlnemjlizçutl.

Auh ynjc itoca, ixcujna: qujl navinti eoah, in cioa: ynjc ce ytoca tiacapan, ynjc vme, ytoca teicu, ynjc ey, itoca tlaco: ynjc nauj itoca xocutzin. Jnjque hin, naujntin cioa: qujl teteu. Jnjque hin, ceceiaca yntoca: tlaçulteteu.

Auh ynjc motocaiotia tlahelquanj: qujl ipampa, imixpã mjtoa, imjxpan mopoa, yn jxqujch nequalli: iixpan mjtoa, momelaoa, yn jxqujch tlahellachioalli: immanel cenca temamauhti, immanel cenca oujh: atle mopinavizcaoa, vel muchi, iixpan neci, ixpan mjtoa.

Neiolmelaoaliztli.

Qujlmach in tlaçulli, in teuhtli, in aujlnemjliziotl: iehoatl qujtemaca, ic temotla, ic tehipitza in tlaçulteutl. Auh çan no iehoatl, qujtepolhuja: iehoatl chico, tlanaoac qujujca, qujteca: iehoatl, tepapaca, tehaltia: iehoatl imac manj ym matlalatl, in toxpalatl.

67. *Avilnemizyotl* in *Real Palacio MS.*

68. Cf. Eduard Seler, *Tonalamatl of the Aubin Collection,* p. 93: "It is the goddess who is by the interpreters called *Ixcuina,* 'she of two faces' or 'of two-colored face,' and Tlaçolteotl, 'Goddess of Dirt,' and is explained as goddess of lust, of sensual love, and as patroness of adulterers.... She, this goddess, or these goddesses — for under the designation *Ixcuinan,* she was thought of as in the plural number, and, indeed, as stated by Sahagún in his first book as four sisters of different age — was the deity who, according to this legend, introduced the peculiar kind of sacrifice which was offered to the earth — the shooting to death with arrows." The names of these four sisters were common girls' names.

69. Sahagún's corresponding Spanish is *"comedora, de cosas suzias."*

70. In *Real Palacio MS, neiolmelaoaliztli* stands alone as a heading, as given here. In the *Florentine Codex,* it is part of the text.

71. Cf. Seler, *op. cit.,* p. 57, discussing Chalchiuhtlicue and Tlaçolteotl: "... the water ... is not only emblematic of the mutability and evanescence of earthly being, in that it sweeps away all things, but is also the symbol of purification and cleansing; it removes filth, which is sin. Thus speaks the midwife when four days after its birth she subjects the child to a ceremonious washing: 'My son, come unto thy Mother, the Goddess of Water, *Chalchiuhtlicue.* May she cleanse thee of the dirt which thou hast of thy father and thy mother'.... 'My son, come unto thy Mother, thy Father, the Lady *Chalchiuhtlicue,* the Lord *Chalchiuhtlatonac* ... enter the water, the blue (*Matlalac*), the yellow (*Tozpalac*), may it wash thee, may it cleanse thee perfectly, may it take from thee the evil which thou hast from the beginning of the world, which clings to thee from thy father, from thy mother.' " Sahagún (Garibay, ed., Vol. II, p. 188), notes "... *oraciones con que la partera oraba a la diosa del agua llamada* Chalchiuhtlícue *y* Chalchiuhtlatónac, *y decía así: 'Señora nuestra* Chalchiuhtlícue *y* Chalchiuhtlatónac, *venido ha a vuestra presencia esta criatura: ruégoos que la recibáis.' Dicho esto la partera tomaba el agua echaba sobre ella su resuello, y luego la daba*

And thus she pardoned, thus she set aside, she removed [corruption]. In her presence confession was made, the heart was opened; before Tlaçolteotl one recited, one told one's sins.

Auh injc qujtepopolhuja, ynjc chico, tlanaoac, qujujca, qujteca: iixpan neiolcujtilo, iixpan neiolmelaoalo, yn tlaçulteutl, iixpã mopoa, mjhtoa, in tetlachioal.

And her mediator,[72] the one who became her hearer, was the soothsayer, the wise one, in whose hands lay the books, the paintings; who preserved the writings,[73] who possessed the knowledge, the tradition, the wisdom which hath been uttered.

Auh iix, ynacaz, ytlacaccauh muchioa, in tlapouhquj, in tlamatinj, yn jmac manj, yn amuxtli, yn tlacujlolli: in qujpia yn tlilli, yn tlapalli, yn matile yn piale, yn nonotzale, yn oqujto

The penitent who would confess first explained to the soothsayer; he said unto him: "I wish to go to the master, our lord of the near, the nigh,[74] our lord the night, the wind. I wish to learn of his secrets."[75]

yn mojolmelaoaz in tlapilchioale; achto qujtlacaqujtia, in tlapouhquj, qujlhuja. Ca ytechtzinco njnaxitiznequj, yn tlacatl, yn totecujo, in tloque naoaque: in totecujo, yioalli, yn ehecatl, ytoptzin, ypetlacaltzin, njcnottitiliznequj.

The soothsayer said: "Thou has done a favor."

Qujlhuja in tlapouhquj: otimotlacnelili:

He instructed him when he should come; he chose the day. He consulted his sacred almanac, he noted the good day, the good time, the favorable time. It is said that he chose the day.

qujnaoatia, yn iqujn oallaz: qujpepena in tonalli, qujtta yn jamux, yn jtlacujlol: qujtta, yn iqujn qualli tonalli, yn ieccan, in qualcan: mjtoa: qujtonalpepenja.

And when it was already the appointed time, he bought a new reed mat, and incense, and wood. When the penitent was highly honored, he made his confession in his own house; the soothsayer went there. Or perchance the penitent went to him.

Auh yn ie yquac, in ie ynaoatilpan, iancujc petlatl quicoa: yoan copalli, yoan quaujtl: yn tlamauizti in tlamaceuhquj, çan ichan yn moiolmelaoa, ie vmpa iauh in tlapouhquj. Auh anoce teujc iauh, in tlamaceuhquj:

He swept well the place where the new reed mat was placed, and a fire was lit. Then the soothsayer cast the incense into the flames. He addressed the fire; he said:

iancujc petlatl in moteca, vellachpano yn vncan motlalia; yoan tletlalilo: njman copalli contema in tleco in tlapouhquj, qujnotza in tletl; qujlhuja.

"Mother of the gods, father of the gods, the old god, here hath come a man of low estate.[76] He cometh here weeping, sad, anguished. Because[77] he hath sinned, because he hath erred, because he hath lived in filth, it causeth him sorrow, anguish. Master, our

Teteu ynnan, teteu ynta, veue teutl, njcan oallatia in cujtlapilli, yn atlapalli, yn maceoalli: njcan chocatiujtz, tlaocuxtiujtz, moteupouhtiujtz, ancan omalauh, ancan omotepotlamj, ancan oqujnamjc yn vitlallotl, in tocatzaoalli, yn çacamjtl; a qujiolitlacoa,

---

a gustar a la criatura, y también la tocaba el pecho con ella, y el celebro de la cabeza, a manera de cuando se pone el óleo y crisma a los niños, y decíale de esta manera: 'Hijo mío muy amado — y si era mujer decía, hija mía muy amada —, llegaos a vuestra madre y padre la señora Chalchiuhtlícue *y* Chalchiuhtlatónac; *tómeos ella, porque ella os ha de llevar a cuestas y en los brazos en este mundo. Y luego metía en el agua a la criatura, y decía: 'Entra hijo mío — o hija mía —, en el agua, que se llama* matlálac *y* tuxpálac; *láveos en ellas, límpieos él que está en todo lugar, y tenga por bien de apartar de vos todo mal que traéis con vos desde antes del principio del mundo.'"* Seler (*loc. cit.*) establishes a connection between Chalchiuitl icue and Tlaçolteotl. In the fifth week of the *Tonalamatl of the Aubin Collection*, which is ruled over by Chalchiuitl icue, the water goddess holds the head of Tlaçolteotl in her hand. In the *Codex Borbonicus* for the corresponding fifth week, a stream of water issues from the throne of the water goddess and in the current is the headdress of Tlaçolteotl. These two illustrations motivated Seler's remarks on the relationship between the two.

72. See *Florentine Codex*, Book VI, Chap. 43.

73. Cf. *Florentine Codex*, Book VI, Chap. 43.

74. Cf. Corresponding Spanish text. Sahagún (Garibay ed.), Vol. I, p. 88, and Vol. II, p. 81, gives as meanings of *yoalli, ehecatl* (1) *"espíritu, aire y tiniebla"*; and (2) *"dios invisible, sin imagen ... impalpable, y favorecedor y amparador y todopoderoso, por cuya virtud todos viven ..."* Ángel María Garibay K., *Llave del náhuatl* (Otumba, Mexico: Imprenta Mayli, 1940), p. 113, translates *tloque naoaque* as *"que está cerca y junto"* — the sun, God in general.

75. Cf. *Florentine Codex*, Book VI, Chap. 43.

76. Cf. *Florentine Codex*, Book, VI, Chap. 43.

77. *Anca* in *Real Palacio MS.*

lord of the near, the nigh, receive, hear the torment of this lowly one."

Then the soothsayer spoke unto him who would confess; he said unto him:

"Thou hast brought thyself into the presence of him of the near, the nigh. Thou hast come to tell him, to deliver thyself of, thy evil atmosphere, thy corruption. Thou hast come to open thy secrets.

"No more shalt thou err or sin. Before him of the near, the nigh, our lord the night, the wind, take off thy clothing, show thy nakedness.

"Wilt thou see our lord as a man, and[78] will he, as a man, address thee, for he is the night, the wind [for he is invisible, for he is the night, the wind]?[79]

"But in whatever manner thou comest, uncover thy secrets, tell thy way of life, thy deeds, in whatsoever way thou art moved, in whatsoever manner it is, whatsoever thou hast done, whatsoever thou hast achieved, whatsoever thou dost which is evil and sinful.

"Overturn, pour forth thy vices, thy wrongdoing, thy evil odor, thy corruption, and tell thy sorrows to our lord of the near, the nigh, who stretching forth his arms to thee, embraceth thee and carrieth thee upon his back.

"Be daring; be not timid because of shame; be not backward."

Then the penitent kissed the earth and cast incense upon the fire. Thereupon he seated himself before the soothsayer. He spoke as to a lieutenant, a deputy, a representative.

"Our lord of the near, the nigh, since thou receivest, thou perceivest my evil odor, my vices, I take off my clothing and uncover, in thy presence, my nakedness — [that is] what I have perpetrated, what I have done. Can these things be hidden, can they be darkened, when that which I have perpetrated is reflected, is clear in thy sight?"

Then he began [the tale of] his sins, in their proper order, in the same order as that in which he had committed them. Just as if it were a song, just as he intoned a song, in the very same way he told what he had done. As if on a road he went following his deeds; in the very same manner he went following them.

qujtequjpachoa, Tlacatle, totecujoe, tloquehe naoaquehe, manoço xicmocujli, ma xicmocaqujti, yn jnentlamachiliz yn maceoalli.

Niman qujnotza, yn moiolmelauhquj, in iehoatl tlapouhquj: qujlhuja.

Tioalmovicatia yujctzinco, iixpantzinco, in tloque naoaque; ticmolhujlico, ticmomaqujlico, yn mjiaca, in mopalanca: ticmotlapolhujlico, in motop, im mopetlacal,

a ma no ceppa ieh njcan timatoiauj, timotepexiuj: ma ixpantzinco ximopepetlaoa, ximomamaxauj, in tloque, naoaque, in totecujo, in ioalli, in ehecatl.

A cujx tictlacaittaz in totecujo, a cujx mjtztlacanotzaz: ca ioalli, ca ehecatl.

Auh ynjn quen tiujtz, ma xictlapo im motop, in mopetlacal: ma xicpoa in monemjliz, in motlachioal, yvin quenjn ticmati, yvin quenjn cah: in quenjn muchiuh, in quenjn tax: in quenjn ticchiuh, in monequal, in monequaujtec:

xicnoquj, xicpetlanj, in maiectica, in maqualtica, in mjiaca in mopalanca. Auh xicmotlaoculnonochili, yn totecujo, in tloque naoaque, in momaçoaltitica, y macochetica, in teputzetica;

ximotlapalo, ma timopinoquetz, ma titzicolo.

Nimã õtlalqua in tlamaceuhquj, oncopaltema: njman ixpan motlalia in tlapouhquj: qujlhuja, injc teviujti, ynjc tepatiloti, ynjc teixiptla.

Totecujoe, tloquehe, naoaquehe: ca ticmocujlia, ca ticmocaqujtia, in njiaca in nopalanca: mjxpantzinco, njnopepetlaoa, njnomamaxauja: ca onax, ca onjcchiuh: cujx ichtaca, cujx tlaiooaian, ca tezcac, ca tlavilpan im mjxpantzinco, yn onax.

Niman compeoaltia: in jtlapilchioaliz, vel iujn quenjn cah, vel yujn quenjn qujchiuh: yn maca çan cujcatl, cenca çan jvin coneoa, cencan yvin conjtoa, yn juh qujchjuh, im maca çan vtli, cencan qujtocatiuh yn jtlachioal, yn juhuj cencan qujtocatiuh.

78. *Auh* in *Real Palacio MS*.

79. After *ehecatl, Real Palacio MS* adds *"ca amo ittoni ca yovalli ca ehecatl."* This passage has been inserted in brackets.

And when he ended his words, when he had told all his deeds, then the soothsayer, the one who became the mediator, the lieutenant, the deputy, answered him. He said unto him:

"Behold, thou hast spoken to him of the near, the nigh, thou hast offered him thy deeds, thy misdeeds.

"And behold, this thou shalt do, this thou shalt accomplish. When the Ciuapipiltin descend, when it is the feast day of the Ciuapipiltin or the Ixcuiname, thou shalt fast four days. Thou shalt starve thy entrails; thou shalt parch thy lips.

"And on the very feast day, when it has come, at night thou shalt pierce thy tongue with straws, thou shalt draw sticks [through it]. With these thou shalt thus repent thy sins. These thou thus payest in blood.

"And whatsoever thou shalt require, so thou shalt require it. If thou piercest thy tongue with straws thou shalt pass through reeds or sticks. And thou shalt pass them either through thy ears or through thy tongue.

"But as thou shalt pass[80] the reeds through thy tongue, take care lest thou do penance only to earn merit; rather, expiate thy sinful life. Thou shalt pierce thy tongue through the middle, thou shalt break it through from the under side. Thou shalt insert [the reeds] in thy penis.

"When thou drawest it through, thou shalt cast it down behind thee. Thou shalt pass them through singly, or pass them through as one, binding them together, be they four hundred or eight hundred sticks which thou shalt pass through.

"Thus shalt thou overcome thy faults, thy sins, thy evil."

And if the sins of the penitent were only light [the soothsayer] said unto him:

"Thou shalt parch thy lips, thou shalt fast, thou shalt starve thy entrails for four days."

Or else he said unto him:

"Thou shalt sing and dance; thou shalt hang rubber-spotted papers and fashion images."[81]

Or else he said unto him:

"Verily thou art at enmity with wine; thou shalt satisfy the Totochtin."

And he said unto him; he thus commanded him:

"When thou goest, when thou dost thy penance at

Auh yn otlamjto yn jtlatol, yn omuchi qujto ytlachioal: qujnanqujlia, yn tlapouhquj, yn jxtli, yn nacaztli muchioa, in teujujti, in tepatilloti: qujlhuja.

O ca ticmononochilia, ca ticmomaqujlia, in tloque naoaque, im motlachioal, in monequavitec.

Auh ynjn, ca izca yn taiz, yn ticchioaz: yn jquac temoa, yn jquac temo cioapipilti, anoçe yn jquac ymjlhujuh cioapipilti, yn jxcujname: naujlujtl timoçaoaz, timocujtlaxculçaoaz, timotenoatzaz.

Auh yn iquac vel jlhujtl, in ie oallatujh, in ioaltica tiçacatlaçaz, titlacoqujxtiz: ynjn motlapilchioal, iuh ticnamjctiz y: auh ynjn iuh namjque ez y:

auh jn quenjn ticnequiz, iuh ticnequiz: yntla tiçacatlaçaz, iehoatl in teucalçacatl tiqujxtiz, anoço tlacotl. Auh aço monacazco in titlaqujxtiz, anoço monenepilco.

Auh ynjc tiqujxtiz: ca amo ma çan titlamaçeoaz, ca teuhtli, tlaçulli in tictlaça, tictlacoçoz, ticcujtlacueponiz ỹ monenepil, mjxpampa ticaquiz,

motzintlan in ticqujxtiz, in tictlaçaz: aço çan cecen in ticqujxtiz, anoço çan ticcenqujxtiz, tictlatlaçalhuiz, yn aço centzontli, aço vntzontli, in ticqujxtiz tlacotl:

ic poliuiz, in motlatlacul, in motlapilchioal, im monequal.

Auh intla çan xicca, yn jtlapilchioal, tlamaceuhquj: qujlhuja,

timotenoatzaz, titlacatlaquaz, timocujtlaxculçaoaz, naujlhujtl:

anoço qujlhuja

titlatotiz, timoteteuhcaoaz, titepiquiz:

anoço qujlhuja.

ca nel vctli, yn jpan otitlaneçomalti, tiqujnqujxtiz in totochtin.

Auh qujlhuja, ynjc qujnaoatia:

yn iquac tiaz, yn titlamaceoaz ioaltica, atle mo-

80. *Ticquixtiz* in *Real Palacio MS*.

81. Although the *Real Palacio MS* reads *timoteteuhçavaz*, the corresponding Spanish text favors the present translation.

night, thou shalt wear nothing. Thou shalt go naked. About thy loins will go placed a paper painted with obsidian points;[82] one piece will go placed behind thee, at thy buttocks.

"And when thou shalt return, there before our lords, the gods, thou shalt cast off thy paper skirt."

And when he had done his penance, then he went to his house.

Thus in the end he changed his way of life. It was said that if he were to sin again — so it was said — no more might he gain mercy therefor.

It was said that they told only of great faults, grave misdeeds, adultery, [and only] the aged so spoke.

Thus the aged confessed — it was said — that they might not be punished here on earth for their sins; if they had committed adultery, so that their heads might not be pierced, nor crushed, nor beaten with stones, [therefore] they confessed.

The soothsayer before whom sins were laid nowhere spoke of what had been placed before him, of what had been said. For what was said, what was confided, was not to him. For the sins were given — they were told — to him of the near, the nigh, whom mortal man might not see.

tech vetztiaz, tipetlauhtiaz: yn momaxac, amatl tlaitzcopeoalli in mantiaz: centetl mjcampa, motzintlampa, mantiaz.

Auh yn jquac tioalmocuepaz, vmpa tocontlaçaz yn jmjxpan totecujooan, yn teteu, ym mamacue.

Auh yn jquac otlamaceuh, njman oalauh yn jchan:

ic cenmajan, monemjlizcuepa: qujlmach intla oc cepa tlatlacoz, qujl ça aocmo tlaoculilonj.

Qujlmach çan yio vey nequalli, vey nequaujtectli, in tetlaximaliztli: in qujtoaia veuetque.

Jnjc moiolmelaoaia veuetque: qujlmach, iehoatl, ynjc amo tzacujltilozque, njcan tlalticpac, yn jntlapilchioal: yntla otetlaxin: ynjc amo quatetlaxililoz, ynjc amo quatepitzinjloz, ynjc amo quatetzotzonaloz, moiolmelaoa.

Jn tlapouhqui, yn jixpan tlalilo, tlapilchioalli: çan njman acan qujtoa, in tlein ixpan tlalilo, in tlein ilhujlo: ipampa ca amo ieh yn jlhujlo, in nonotzalo, ca tloque, ca naoque, in maco, in jlhujlo, in tlapilchioalli: ca amo ieh motta, im maceoalli.

82. The most characteristic emblem of Tlaçolteotl is a broom wrapped with a *tlaitzcopintli* — paper impressed with pointed figures (see *Codex Borbonicus,* month of Ochpaniztli). The paper loin cloth is no doubt of this same pattern. Probably the *huipil* worn by the goddess in the illustration (Pl. 12) is a good indication of the design of the loin cloth.

Thirteenth Chapter, which telleth of the lesser gods[83] who follow the principal gods which have been mentioned.

Xiuhtecutli (Turquoise Lord), Ixoçauhqui (Yellow-faced One), and Cueçaltzin (Flaming One). This one was known as the fire or Ueue teotl (the Old God) and Tota (Our Father).

He was thought a god, considering that he burned one, he consumed one, he singed one, he scorched the fields. And for many purposes was he useful; for with him one was warmed, things were cooked in an olla, things were cooked, things were toasted, salt [water] was evaporated, syrup was thickened, charcoal was made, limestone was fired; things were well fried; things were fried, things were roasted; one was burned, sweat-houses were heated, unguents were prepared, the lime preparation for renovating capes was heated.

And when his feast day was celebrated, once a year, at the end of the month of Izcalli, they made an image of Moctezuma; before it quail were beheaded and incense was set forth.

Tamales [stuffed] with greens[84] were prepared in each dwelling. First they were placed before the fire. Then they were eaten.

And all day his [the god's] old men sang, blew shell trumpets,[85] beat horizontal drums, sounded the rattle-board for him.

And no one might reach his hand[86] to the griddle. It was forbidden that anyone burn himself, singe himself, because tamales [stuffed] with greens which had been offered were eaten for the first time.

Jnic matlactli vmey, capitulo: yntechpa tlatoa, yn tepitoton teteuh: yn qujntoqujlia, yn omoteneuhque, yn veueintin teteuh.

Xiuhtecutli: ixcoçauhquj, yoan cueçaltzin. Jehoatl motocaiotia in tletl, anoço veue teutl yoan tota:

teutl ipan machoia: iehica, ca tetlatia, tepaloa, techichinoa, tlachinoa: yoan mjec tlamantli, ynjc tlacnelia: ca ic nezcolo, ic tlapaoaxo, ic tlacuxitilo, ic tlaxco, ic iztatlatilo, ic necutlatilo, ic tecullatilo, ic tenextlatilo, ic tlatetzoionjlo, yc tlatzoionjlo, ic tlatleoatzalo, yc tetlecujlolo, ic temazcallatilo, ic oxitlatilo, ic tlanextlatilo.

Auh yn iquac ilhujqujxtililoia, cexiuhtica: ipan itlamjan yzcalli: qujxiptlatiaia in motecuçuma, ixpan tlacotonaloia, copaltemjlilo,

oauhqujltamalli nechivililoia, in cecencalpan: achto ixpan qujmanjliaia in tletl, çatepan qualoia.

Auh yn jveveiooan, iuh cemjlhujtl, in qujcujcatia, qujteccizpichilia, qujteponacilhuja, caiacachilhuja:

auh aiac vel cõmaçoaia in comalco, tetlacaoaltiloia, ynjc amo aca motlatiz, mochichinoz: ipampa in iancujcan oqualoc oauhqujltamalli, ynjc otlamanaloc.

83. Corresponding Spanish text has: *"que son menores en dignjdad, que los arriba dichos."*

84. *"Una de las hierbas que se comen cocidas se llama* huauhquílitl, *que son bledos; es muy verde, tiene las ramas delgadillas y altillas, tiene las hojas anchuelas. Los tallos de esta hierba se llaman* huauhtli *(y) la semilla se llama de la misma manera; esta hierba se cuece para comer, sabe a cenizos, exprímese del agua que se cuece para comerse; hácense tamales de esta hierba, los cuales se llaman* quiltamalli" (Sahagún, *op. cit.*, Vol. III, p. 295).

85. *Quiteuccizpichilia* in *Real Palacio MS.*

86. *Uellonmaçouaya* in *ibid.*

And all the little children[87] roasted some snakes, frogs, small white fish, the axolotl, birds; whatsoever kind of small animal they had captured, they cast in the hearth. Thus, they said: "Our father roasteth [something] for himself."

Auh in pipiltotonti, muchintin qujntlaxqujaia: yn aca coatl: cujiatl, xoujli, axolotl, tototl: in çaço tlein ocacic ioioli, ycamac contlaçaia in tlecujlli: ic mjtoaia, motlaxquja yn tota.

And when night fell, in all places the old men, the old women drank wine. They made libations to the fire, they extinguished the oven[88] — so they said.

Auh yn oiooac, noujan tlatlaoanaia in vevetque, ylamatque: iuh qujtoaia, qujtlatoiaujliaia yn tletl, texcalceuja.

And every four years his feast day was especially honored. Moctezuma then danced a princely dance before the temple of Xiuhtecutli. The name of the place was Tzonmolco.[89]

Auh nauhxiuhtica, yn oc cenca, mauiztililoia, ilhuiuh: iquac motecujtotiaia yn motecuçuma, ixpan yn jteucal, xiuhtecutli, ytocaiocan tzonmulco.

And at this time all people, everyone, tasted, sipped the wine; [also] the small children. Thus the [feast day] was called *pillaoano.*

Auh in jquac hy, vel muchitlacatl, vel no ixqujch tlacatl, qujpaloaia, qujltequja, in vctli, in pipiltotonti: ic motocaiotiaia, pillaoano:

And then they gave uncles, they gave aunts to the small children, a man, a woman whom those with children sought out and gave gifts. These took [the children] upon their backs, and then carried[90] them to the temple of Ixcoçauhqui. There [the parents] perforated their ears, they pierced their ears; thus they placed a sign upon them, while their uncles and aunts[91] looked on. Afterwards food was eaten.[92]

yoan vncã qujntlatiaia, qujnmahujtiaia in pipiltotonti. Ce cioatl, ce oqujchtli, in qujntemoaia pilhoaque, qujntlauhtiaia, iehoantin qujnmamatihuja, vmpa qujmoncaoaia, yn iteupan ixcoçauhquj: vmpa qujnnacazxapotlaia, qujnnacazcoionjaia: iuhqujn ic qujnmachiotiaia, ynjc qujmitta, yntlaoan, ymaujoan: çatepan tlaqualo.

His array was [thus]: black was smeared about the lower part of the face. About his head he bore a circlet set with green stones;[93] he wore a paper crown with the feathers of the lovely cotinga and a spray of quetzal feathers; he had a crown of arrowshafts, a crown of spearshafts; he had the fire-serpent disguise;[94] he had a shoulder-sash of yellow paper.[95] Likewise he had bells, he had shells. His shield had pieces of turquoise and mirror-stone. He carried the staff with the device for seeing.

Jn jnechichioal catca: tliltica motenujltec, chalchiuhtetele, xiuhtotoamacale, quetzalmjiaoaio, mjtzone, tlacotztzone, xiuhcooanacoche, amacozneapanale, no tzitzile, cocujole, xiuhtezcatlatlapanquj yn jchimal, tlachieltopile.

---

87. In the corresponding Spanish text, the children's parents hunted and roasted these animals. In Sahagún (Garibay ed., Vol. I, p. 220), we are told that the old men received the animals from the children as offerings and threw the offerings in the fire.

88. *Texcalceuja*: cf. *op. cit.*, p. 221; *"dar refrigerio al fogón"* in *ibid.*, Vol. IV, p. 357.

89. Described as the 64th temple in Tenochtitlan (*ibid.*, Vol. I, p. 240).

90. For *quimoncaoaia* the *Real Palacio MS* has *q'mõvicaya.*

91. Corresponding Spanish text uses the word *padrino* (god-father; patron or protector).

92. After *tlaqualo, Real Palacio MS* adds *tlavano* — there was drinking.

93. *Chalchiuhtetel: "un haro con piedras preciosas"* (Sahagún, *op. cit.*, Vol. IV, p. 282).

94. For *xiuhcooanacoche, Real Palacio MS* has *xiuhcoanavale.*

95. *Amacozneapanale:* the *amaneapanalli* is a band of paper which hangs from one's shoulder, the ends crossing under the opposite elbow. See Pl. 20.

Fourteenth Chapter, which telleth of the god named Macuilxochitl (Five Flower) and Xochipilli (Flower Prince).

Likewise he was worshipped as a god of the palace folk.

When there was fasting, if one of us men lay with a woman, or a woman with a man, it was said, "they brought to naught their fasting through sin."

Thereupon [the god] gave them, visited upon them, gave them as their merit, their lot, piles, hemorrhoids, suppurating genitals, disease of the groin.[96]

Therefore vows were made to him,[97] vows were repeated, to quiet, remove, abate the sickness.

And when his feast was celebrated on the feast day of flowers, first there was a flower fast for four days. Some fasted by eating no chili; they ate [only] at midday,[98] they ate [only] once. At midnight they tasted a painted atole which they drank; small flowers floated on it. [When] they flower-fasted, they ate all manner of tasty things; likewise they tasted them at midday. And some ate only one thing—tortillas of maize not softened by lime,[99] without chili. Likewise they tasted them at midday.

On the fifth day, which was when the feast was celebrated, a man made himself into the likeness [of the god]; he placed on himself the array [of the god], in which he danced. They beat the drum and sang for him.

And at midday, quail were beheaded. There were the drawing of blood, the passing of sticks [through

Jnic matlactli vnnavi capitulo: itechpa tlatoa in teutl, yn itoca: macuilxochitl, yoan xochipilli.

Çan neneuhque, ynjc neteutiloia tecpantzinca inteuh:

yn jquac neçaujliloia, intla aca toqujchti ipan cioacochiz, anoço cioatl, ipan oqujchcochiz: mjtoaia, qujntlaçulmjctia, yn jneçaoaliz,

ic quitemacaia, tetech qujtlaliaia, qujteilhujltiaia, qujtemaceoaltiaia, in xochiciuiztli, yn menexoaliztli, tlapalanaltiliztli, quexiliuiliztli,

yuicpa nêtoloa, nenetoltiloia, ynjc qujceuiz, ynjc qujquaniz, ynjc qujcaxaoaz, cuculiztli.

Auh yn jquac ilhujqujxtililoia, ipan xochilhujtl: achtopa navilhujtl nexochiçaoalo: in cequjntin ic moçaoaia, chilcaoaia, qujn nepantla tonatiuh, in tlaquaia, centlaquaia, ioalnepantla qujmattiuh, tlacujlolatulli in qujia, xochitontli yn ipan ca, moxochiçaoa: muchi qujqua in velic, çan no nepantla tonatiuh qujmattiuh. Auh yn aca çan qujxcaviaia, in iotlaxcalli qujquaia, atle chilli: no nepantla tonatiuh qujmattiuh:

yc tlamacujlti yn jlhujqujxtililoia, iquac ce tlacatl qujmixiptlatiaia, conmaqujaia yn jtlatquj, ipan mjtotiaia, qujtlatzotzonjliaia, qujcujcatiaia:

yoan in ie nepantla tonatiuh, tlacotonaloia, neçuoaia, tlacoqujxtiloia: yoã tlamanjliloia yn jteupan,

96. Corresponding Spanish text reads: *"herja, con emfermedades, de las partes secretas,... almorranas, pudredumbre del miembro secreto, deviesos, y incordios, etc."*

97. *Netoloa: nêtoloya* in *Real Palacio MS.*

98. *Quinnepantla: yn inepantla* in *ibid.*

99. In corresponding Spanish text: *"panes azimos."*

the tongue], and the setting out of offerings in his temple. They made for him five tamales called fasting food. They were very large. On them stood the flowery arrow.

Some thus offered their offering upon wooden plates, and followed it with five more small tamales with a sauce. And [they offered] two cakes of amaranth seed dough, which served in place of rubber, one black, one red, resting in wooden bowls.

And some [offered] toasted maize, or toasted maize mixed in honey,[100] or S-shaped tortillas, butterfly-shaped tortillas, tortillas of maize not softened in lime, tortillas of amaranth seed dough, amaranth seed dough cakes in the form of shields, arrows, swords, dolls.

And here, to Mexico, from everywhere, were brought captives, called "tribute-captives." All who lay surrounding, those who held the enemy borders, those who dwelt on the enemy borders brought their captives, their prisoners here. [These] became their tribute-captives. The stewards, each of the stewards, guarded them here.

And if one of them fled, if he escaped, they replaced him; a man was purchased; they delegated another, they placed one in his stead.

Then the slaves died, when the feast day was celebrated.

And his array [was thus]: on his lips was the imprint of a hand. His face was a fine red; his face glowed red, reddened. He had a crown of feathers, a crest. A fan was the burden on his back, on which stood the sun-flag, with quetzal feathers at the top, with a quetzal feather tuft at the top. His loins were girt by a cloth edged in red. He wore sun sandals.

macujltetl in qujchiujliaia, tamalli: mjtoaia tlacatlaqualli, cenca vevey ipan ycatiuh xuchmjtl:

yn aca quauhcaxitl ynjc conmanjliaia, yoan contoqujliaia oc no macuiltetl tamaltepitoton, mollotiuja: yoan vntetl tzoalli yiol poujia, no cecnj quauhcaxtica, mantivia, centetl tliltic, centetl tlatlauhquj.

Auh yn aca izqujtl, anoço necuzqujtl, anoço xonecujlli, papalotlaxcalli, iotlaxcalli, tzooallaxcalli, tzoalchimalli, tzooalmjtl, tzooalmaquaujtl, tzooalnenetl:

yoan noujian oalcaoaloia, in mamalti njcan mexico, moteneoa maltequjme, yn jxqujch techiaoalotoc, yn iautenoaque, yn iaotenco onoque, qujnoalcaoaia yn jnmalhoan, yn jntlaaxioan, in maltequjhoan, muchioaia: njcan qujnpiaia, yn calpixque, in cacalpixque.

Auh intla aca tlaielti, intla tlachololti, ypan tlacaquetzaia, motlacacoujaia, qujxiptlaiotiaia, qujxiptlatiaia:

in tlatlacuti, vncan miqujia, yn jquac ilhujqujxtililoia.

Auh yn jnechichioal: tenmacpale ixtlapaloatzale, tlaixtlapaloatzalujlli, tlaixtlapalhvilli, yhujtzoncale, quachichiqujle, vitonquj yn jtlamamal, vitoncatlamamale, ypan icac, tonalopanjtl, quetzaltzonio, quetzaltzontecomaio, quetzaltzontecome, quetzaltzonteconio, tentlapaltica motzinjlpi, motzinapa, ytonalocac, tonalocaque.

100. *Necuzquitl* reads *necuizquitl* in *Real Palacio MS.*

ILLUSTRATIONS

gun demonio: todo esto dezian, que acon
tecia, porque estos dioses, de que aquj
se trata, se aujan enojado contra el.
Despues de acabada la fiesta, otro dia
luego de mañana, el que auja hecho,
la fiesta: juntauan asus parientes,
y asus amigos, y alos de su barrio, cõ
todos los de su casa: y acabauan de
comer, y beuer, todo lo que auja so
brado, de la fiesta. A esto llamavan,
apeoalo, que quiere dezir: añadidura,
alo que estaua comjdo, y beujdo: nin
guna cosa quedaua de comer, nj de be
uer, para otro dia. Dezian que los
gotosos, haziendo esta fiesta, sanauã
de la gota: o de qualesquiera, de las
enfermedades, que arriba se dixerõ:
y los que aujan escapado, de algun
peligro de agua: con hazer esta fies
ta, cumplian con su voto. Acabada
toda la fiesta: los papeles, y adere
ços, conque aujan adornado, estas y
magines: y todas las vasijas, que
aujan sido menester, para el combite:
tomauanlo todo, y lleuauanlo, a vn
sumjdero, que esta en la laguna de
mexico: que se llama pantitlan, y
alli lo arrojauan todo.

ichtaca tlapaloaia, ynjtlachtaca
yia inmanel çan tepiton ocon
palo: iuh mjtoaia tennecujltvia
tepantilivia, avic momamana
avic xoquivi ynite: yoan inaca
matzicoliujia. yma quijcuec
cuetza, ic xi quicuecuetza, ma
copichauj, ic xicopichauj, icxi
cuecuechca, yhixatotoco, ten
papatlaca, tenvivitoca, itech
qujneoa: mjtoa, oqujtlavelique
in xoxouhque tepicme. Auh
ynotlathuje, njman ic ic apeoa
lo: ynapeoa çan iehoan, ynj
cantolque, in vel icalloc, incen
tlaca, cemeoa, in vel icujtlax
colloc, yn vel imecaioc: motene
oa apeoalo, iquac cempoliuja
tlatlamj, in quexqujch mocaoa
ia, in atl, in tlaqualli: yoan inoc
quexqujch omocauh xaxocomje in
vetli, inaiuctli, intlachioalvetli, in
iztacvetli, in cochvetli. Auh ynjte
piqujnj, in tepicquj: in tlacoaci
vi, ynjuh omjto tlacpac, ic patiz:
yoan ynaqujn atlan miquizquja

Page from *Florentine Codex* (Chapter 21)

—*After Paso y Troncoso*

1—Uitzilopochtli. 2—Paynal. 3—Tezcatlipoca. 4—Tlaloc.

—*After Paso y Troncoso*

5—Quetzalcoatl. 6—Ciuacoatl. 7—Chicome coatl. 8—Teteo innan.

—After Paso y Troncoso

9—Tzapotlan tenan. 10—Ciuapipilti. 11—Chalchiuhtli ycue. 12—Tlaçolteotl.

—After Paso y Troncoso

13—Xiuhtecutli. 14—Macuilxochitl or Xochipilli. 15—Omacatl. 16—Ixtlilton.

—*After Paso y Troncoso*

17—Opochtli. 18—Xipe totec. 19—Yiacatecutli. 20—Napa tecutli.

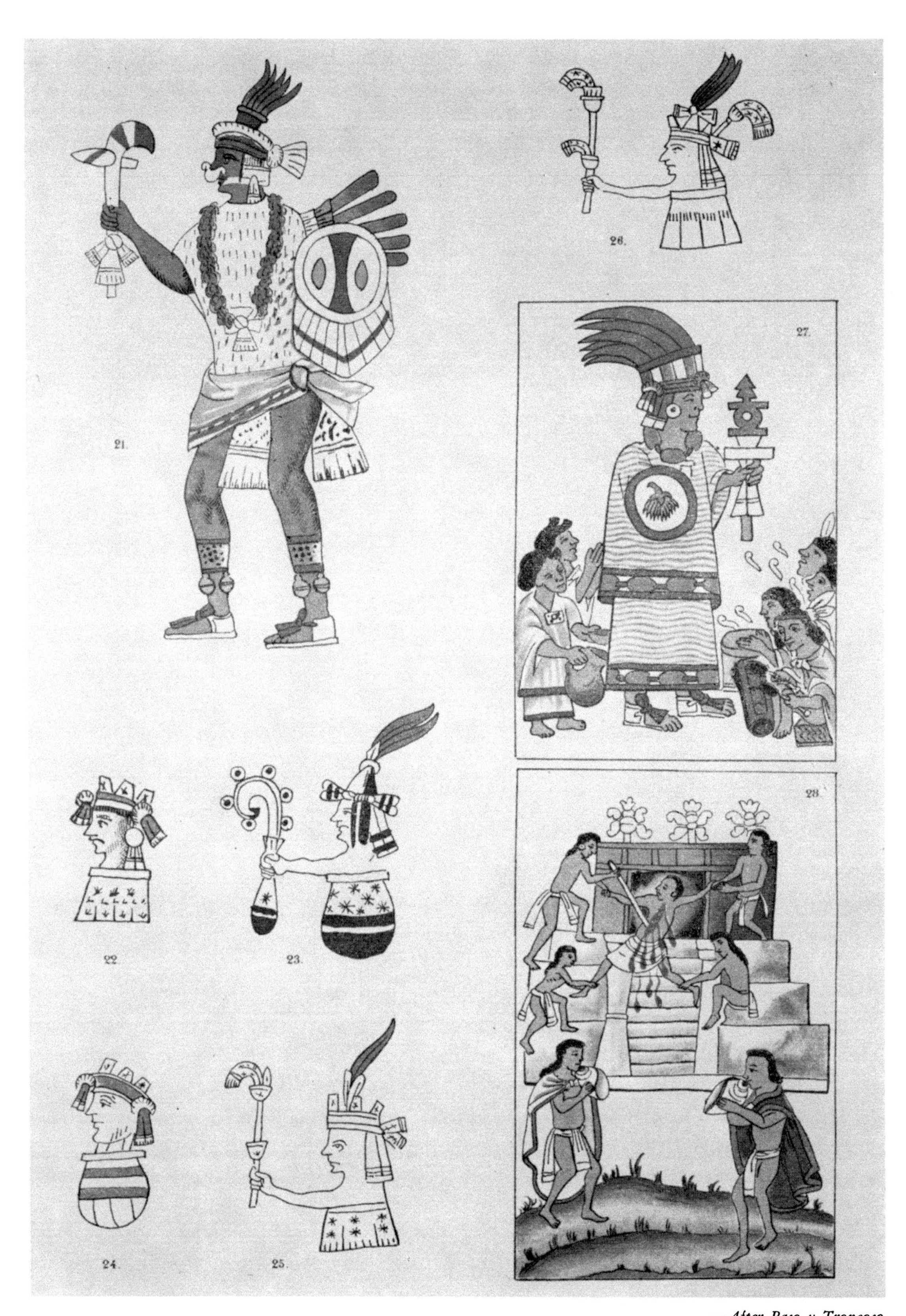

—*After Paso y Troncoso*

21—Tezcatzoncatl. 22–26—Tepictoton (Matlalcueye, Quetzalcoatl, Chalchiuhtli ycue, Popocatepetl, Iztac tepetl) 27—Chalchiuhtli ycue (Chap. 11). 28—Tlalocan (Temple of Tlaloc) (Chap. 11).

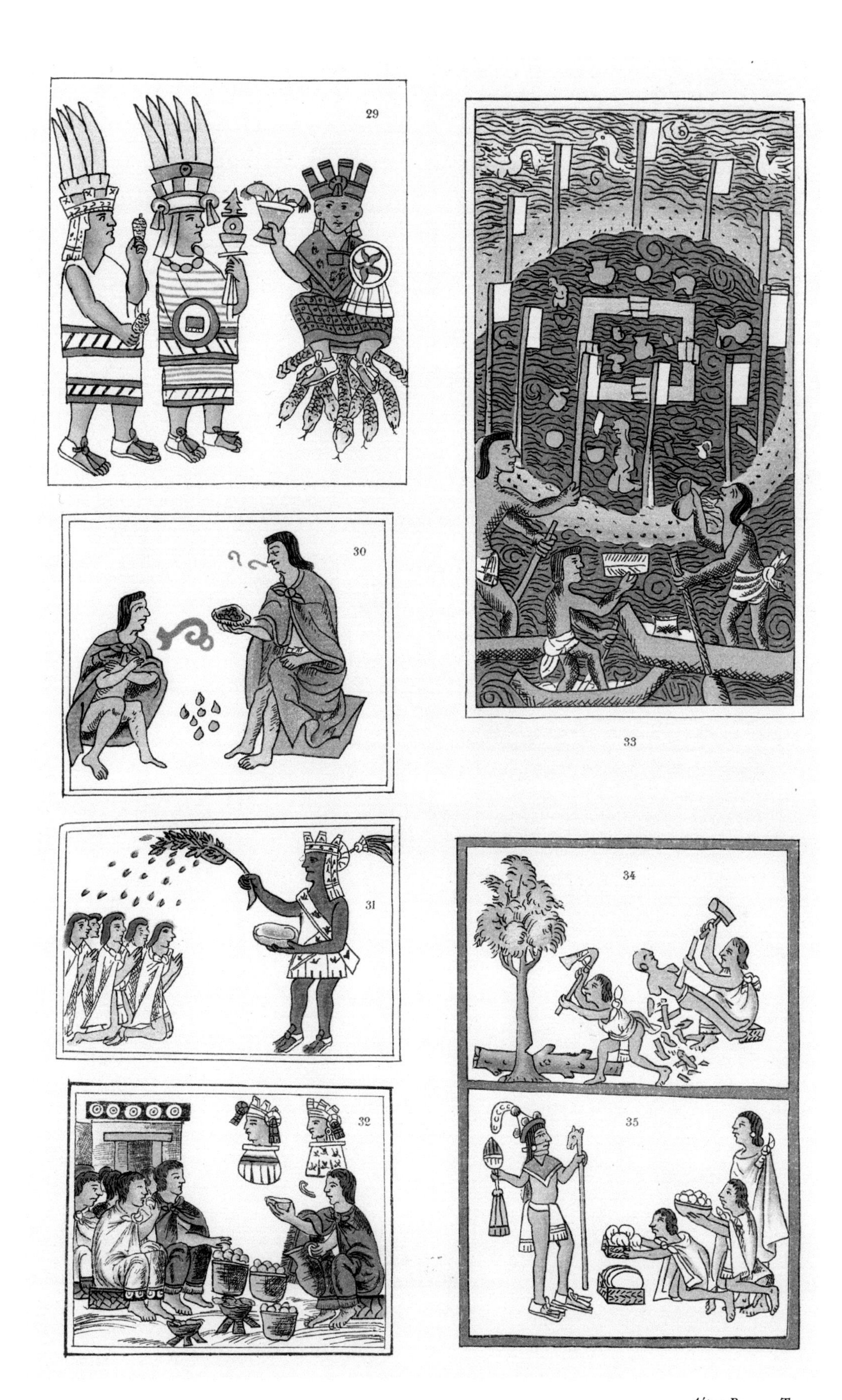

—After Paso y Troncoso

29—Tzapotlan tenan (Chap. 9), Chalchiuhtli ycue (Chap.11), Chicome coatl (Chap. 7). 30—Tlaçolteotl—Confession (Chap. 12). 31—Napa tecutli (Chap. 20). 32—Tepictoton (Chap. 21). 33—Pantitlan (Tepictoton) (Chap. 21). 34—Appendix, Chap. 13. 35—Appendix, Chap. 13.

—*After Paso y Troncoso*

36—Appendix [Confutation]. 37—Appendix [Confutation]. 38—Titlacauan. 39—Xiuhtecutli. 40—Opochtli. 41—Yiacatecutli. 42—Tezcatzoncatl: 43—Tepicme.

Fifteenth Chapter, which telleth of the god named Omacatl (Two Reed).

This Omacatl was god of Uitznauac.[101] To him were attributed, to him were ascribed — they said that his inventions were — banqueting, invitations to feasts, acceptance [of invitations], the feasting of people. His domain became the gathering, the assembling of relatives. To one's house was brought his image, there to be held in esteem and cared for.

And also it was said that if he were not held in esteem, like one invited, he would become angered. He chided one in his sleep or in a dream; he said to him who dreamed: "Thou! Why dost thou not esteem me? I shall depart from thee. Already I know what I shall do to thee."

And if he were sorely enraged, when one ate he often caused him to swallow a hair which was in the drink, in the food. And when, [as] is said, he ate the god, often he sickened. Thus he afflicted him: he choked on his food, he choked on his drink, the food stuck in his throat when he ate. And if he walked, he stumbled, tripped, fell.

And thus was his feast day celebrated. He who ate the god first made a sacred cylinder [of dough]: this was the bone of the god. Only a priest, an elder of the *calpulli*, [made it] — a cubit long, fat, cylindrical.

And before it was shared among them, first all ate; there was drinking, the drinking of wine. And when day broke, they stabbed Omacatl in the abdomen and killed him. Then the sacred roll was shared, broken in pieces, divided among them.

When it was eaten, it was as if one had thus been given an obligation; one had been notified, in-

Jnic caxtolli capitulo, ytechpa tlatoa yn teutl, yn jtoca Omacatl.

Jnjn omacatl, vitznaoac, teutl catca, yn jtech tlamjloia, in piqujliloia, qujtooaia ca iehoatl imactia, in cooaiutl, in tecooanotzaliztli, in tetlacamatiliztli, in tetlatlaqualtiliztli: ymatijan muchioaia, yn jnnecentlaliliz, yn jnnecenqujxtiliz teoaiolque, techã vicoia, vmpa mauizmachoia, necujtlaujloia yn jxiptla.

Auh no qujtooaia, yntlacamo maviztililo, yn juhqujma cooanotzalo, tlavelcuja: tecochpa, anoço tecochizpan, teaoaia, qujlhujaia, yn aqujn qujtemjquj. Jn tehoatl tleyca yn amo tinechmavizmati; njmitztlalcahuiz: auh ie ne njcmati, in tlein mopan njcchioaz.

Auh intla cenca moçuma, yn jquac tlaqualo, mjecpa tzontli qujtetololtia: in atl, in tlaqualli ipan. Auh yn aquĩ yn mjtoa teuqua, miecpa mococoa: ynjc qujtolinja, melcima, ycopac mjlacatzoa in atl: meltepotlamja in jquac tlaqua: auh yntla nenemj, motepotlamja, motecujnja, motlavitequj.

Auh ynjc ilhujqujxtililoia: yn aqujn teuqua, achtopa qujchioaia, teumjmilli, yiomjio in teutl catca: çan tlacatl, teupixquj calpole, cen molicpitl ynjc hujviiac, vel totomaoac, mjmjltic.

Auh yn aiamo nemamaco, oc achtopa tlatlaqualo, atlioa, tlaoano: auh yn otlathujc, conjtitzopinja, yn omacatl conmjctia: njman ic nemamaco, netlatlapanjlo, nexexelhujlo, in teumjmjlli:

iquac quaqualo, iuhqujn ic tetzoiotiloia, tetlacaqujtilo, tetlalhujlo, temolcaoaltilo: ca yn aquique ma-

101. *Vitznauac: ". . . tiene varios significados en náhuatl:*

"i) *'cerca de las espinas.' Es el nombre del sitio que estaba a la vista del altar y en donde se colocaban las espinas del sacrificio ritual que hacían todos, grandes y chicos, al amanecer, al mediar el día y al mediar la noche. Como la disposición de los altares era hacia el sur, por una transición muy fácil de significado, vino a ser el nombre de la zona meridional, tanto la tierra, como en el cielo.*

"ii) *Un sitio de adoración colocado en el rumbo meridional en los pueblos de cultura nahuatl. Hallamos este nombre en diversas poblaciones de esta filiación cultural. Recuerdo al azar, Tezcoco, Otumba, Azcapotzalco, etc. En Tenochtitlan tenemos bien localizado este sitio en el rumbo meridional, en el barrio que los conquistadores llamaron después San Pablo, como es conocido hasta hoy."* (Garibay, *Viente Himnos Sacros de los Nahuas*, p. 42).

formed; it had been verified to one[102] that those to whom it had been given, at the coming of the [next] feast day, paid with their entrails; they made repayments because of the debt.

coia, yn iquac ie ilhujuhqujçaz, mocujtlaxcolixtlaoaia, mopopooaia, ypampa ca ontlaxtlaoaia.

And his array was [thus]: he had a crown of feathers; his was the warrior's crown. His warrior's cape was red-bordered, with eyelets.[103] He had a cape of netting with snail shells.[104] His breast ornament had snail shells. He had fragments of mirrorstone [painted] on his face as his adornment. He wore his chalky ear plug. His shield was chalky; it had paper streamers. The device for seeing was in his hand. His was a stool of reeds, of rushes.

Jn inechichioal catca: ihvitzoncale, quauhtzoncale, yoã yquauhquententenchil, naoaio, ycuechin, ielpancozqui cyli, tezcatlatlapanquj yn jxaiac: yn jnechichioal, ytiçanacoch, ytiçachimal, amapaio, ytlachiaia ymac catca, ytolicpal, acacpalli.

---

102. *Temolcaoaltilo*: in *Real Palacio MS, temelcaualtilo.* The context favors reading as *temelauatilo.* The corresponding Spanish text reads: *"Y todos estos, que aquj, comulgauan, se tenian por dicho, y entendido: que el año que venja, en esta fiesta, aujan de contribuyr: para hazer la fiesta, deste dios: proueyendo todo, lo necessarjo, que se auja de gastar en ella."*

103. *Yquauhquententenchil, naoaio*: in *Real Palacio MS, yquauhquẽ, tenchilnavayo.*

104. *Ycuechin: "... llevaba en las espaldas un ornamento de un palmo en cuadro hecho de tela rala, el cual llamaban* ycuéchin, *atado con cuerdas de algodón a los pechos"* (Sahagún, Garibay ed., Vol. I, p. 160). *"Traía una manta cubierta como red, que llamaban* cuechintli" (*ibid.*, p. 218). For description, see illustrations and text in Seler: *Gesammelte Abhandlungen*, Vol. II, pp. 515 and 523; and also illustration (Omacatl), Pl. 15.

Sixteenth Chapter, which telleth of the god named Ixtlilton (Little Black Face), Tlaltetecuin (the Earth-stamper).[105]

He was a god whose temple was made entirely of wood, at a place named Tlacuilocan. Here in his temple were many earthen tubs, covered over. These were called "his black water."

And whenever a child sickened, they brought him to the temple of Ixtlilton. They uncovered one of the tubs and had him drink "his black water." Thereupon the child became whole.

And when one would arrange a dance, amid incense he went and brought the image of the god to his house — only a man so arrayed.

And when he arrived at his house, there would be dancing. Then all ate; there was drinking. After the eating, then Ixtlilton danced. After he had danced, he entered into the house; he uncovered the wine, which for four days had been covered. This was called the first opening or tapping of the new wine.[106]

Then they began to drink. Again they went out into the court; they uncovered "his black water," which also had been covered for four days. On the fifth day they uncovered it. It was said, it was affirmed, that if dirt, cobwebs, a hair, charcoal lay fallen there, then it was said he was either an adulterer or a thief; or he lived dissolutely, or he lived in vice; or he was a monster, he who had arranged the dance. Thus they confronted and reproached him openly. It was said that he sowed discord among people by reproaching, confronting, threatening people with their sins.

And when [the impersonator] departed from one's house, they gave him a large mantle called *ixquen* (face-covering).[107]

Jnic castolli vce capitulo ytechpa tlatoa, in teutl yn jtoca, catca, ixtlilton, tlaltetecujn.

Teutl catca, çan quavitl yn jteupan catca, ytocaiocan tlacujlocan: in vncan yteupan, mjec yn apaztli, tzatzacutimanca, motocaiotia itlilauh.

Auh yn aqujn mococoaia, piltontli, vmpa qujujcaia yn jteupan ixtlilton: centetl, qujtlapoaia yn apaztli, conjtiaia yn jtlilauh; ic patia in piltontli.

Auh yn aqujn qujtotiz, copaltica in conanaia, ynjc qujvicaia ychan yn jxiptla: çan tlacatl in muchichioaia.

Jn oacic ychan, tlatotiz, teytotiz: njman tlatlaqualo, atlioa: yn otlaqualoc, njman mjtotia, yn jxtlilton: yn omjtoti, yn onmaceuh, calitic oncalaquj: iehoatl qujtlapoa in vctli, navilhujtica tzacutimãca: ic mjtoaia, tlaiacaxapotla, vitzmana.

Niman yc vmpeoa, yn ie tlaoano: oc cepa oalqujça itoalco, qujtlapoa yn jtlilauh, no tzacutimanca navilhujtica: ic macujlilhujtl in qujtlapoa: ic mjtoaia, ic moteneoaia, intla tlaçolli, yntla tocatzaoalli, yntla tzontli, intla tecolli, vncan vetztoc: ic mjtoaia, aço tetlaxima, aço ichtec, anoço ahavilnemj, mahaviltia: ac aço tlacacemelle, in tlatotia, ic qujxmotlaia, qujxcomacaia, qujxpantia: ic mjtoaia, tetzalan, tenepantla moteca: iehica, ca qujteixcomaca, qujteixpantia, ic teixmotla, yn tetlatlacul.

Auh ynjc oalquiça techã, quachtli yn qujmacaia motocaiotia, ixquen.

105. Tlaltetecuin: *"Que salta hiriendo la tierra"* (Sahagún, *op. cit.*, Vol. IV, p. 363).

106. *Ibid.*, Vol. I, p. 326: ". . . *los que nuevamente horadaban los magueyes y hacían vino nuevo, que se llamaba* uitztli." The Spanish text of the Florentine Codex explains that *"a este abrimjento, llamavan tlaiacaxapotla, qujere dezir, esto: abrimjento primero, o vino nueuo."* On the meaning of *onmaceuh*, see Sahagún, *op. cit.*, p. 62 (definition of *maceualiztli*).

107. Corresponding Spanish text: ". . . *dauanle mãtas: las quales llamauan, ixquen: que quiere dezir, cubertura de la cara: porque quedaua auergonçado, aquel que auja hecho, la fiesta. . .*"

Thus was [Ixtlilton] arrayed: he was spread over with unguent; his face was covered with soot; about his lips white clay was placed. He had a crest of flint knives with quetzal feathers added. The burden on his back was a fan of red arara feathers. His sun flag stood upon it. His paper shoulder-sash had sun-emblems. Sun-emblems were on his shield. Red was his staff, upon which was a heart. He had a necklace of rock crystal. He had a paper breech-clout. He had bells, he had shells. He wore sun sandals.

Jnic muchichioaia, moçac, mocemjxtlilpopotz, mjxtiçatlatlali, yn jcamapa: tecpaquachichiqujle, quetzallo, cueçalvitonquj yn jtlamamal, ytonalopan ipan icac, totonaloio yn jamaneapan, totonaloio yn jchimal, tlauhio yiollotopil, xopilcuzque, yamamaxtli, tzitzile, coiole, itonalocac.

Seventeenth Chapter, which telleth of the god whose name was Opochtli (Left), whom the natives worshipped in ancient times.

This Opochtli was an aspect of Tlaloc. He was the god of the water folk; they worshipped him.

They said that he invented, he revealed, the net, the atlatl, the trident,[108] the pole for propelling boats, the bird snare — these were his innovations, his inventions.

And when his feast day was celebrated the offering became drink, food, wine, and the cane of maize plants, flowers, tobacco, incense, sweet-smelling herbs. These they spread before him, thus welcoming him. They shook the rattle-boards for him. They strewed popcorn for him which represented hailstones. And also his old men, his old women, the elders of the *calpulli*, made music for him.

His array was [thus]: he wore a paper crown. He was covered with black unguent — a liquid rubber covering. He had a heron-feather headdress with a spray of quetzal feathers. He wore a paper breech-clout. He had a paper shoulder-sash with the sun-emblem.

Jnic castolli vmome capitulo, ytechpa tlatoa, yn teutl, yn itoca catca opuchtli: yn qujmoteutiaia ie uecauh, nican tlaca.

Inin opuchtli, ipan mixeoaia, tlaloc: atlaca inteuh catca, qujmoteutiaia.

Juh qujtoaia, ca iehoatl itlatzintil, ytlanextil, qujnexti, qujteittiti in matlatl, yn atlatl, yn mjnacachalli, yn avictli, tzonvaztli.

Auh yn iquac ilhujqujxtililoia, atl, tlaqualli, vctli, in ventli muchioaia: yoan cintopilli, xuchitl, yietl, copalli, yiauhtli, qujtepeviliaia, ic qujnanamiquja: chicaoaztli concacalachiliaia mumuchitl qujchaiaviliaia: iuhqujn tecivitl povia: no yoã qujcujcatiaia, yn iveveiooan, yn jlamaiooan, calpoleque.

Jn jnechichioal catca: amacale, tlaôçalli, tlaolaltilli, aztatzone, quetzalmjiaoaio, amamaxtle, amaneapanale, tonaloio.

108. ". . . *un dardo de tres puntas que se llama* minacachalli" (Sahagún, *op. cit.*, Vol. III, p. 242). The corresponding Spanish text on Opochtli contains the same information. ". . . *es como fisga, aunque no tiene, sino tres puntas,* [marginal insertion, partly missing: (*o?*) *triangulo* (*co?*)*mo tridente*] *con que hiere, a los peces; y tambien cõ el matan aues.*"

Eighteenth Chapter, which telleth of the god named Xipe totec (Our Lord the Flayed One).[109]

He was the god of the seashore people, the proper god of the Zapotecs.

That which corresponded to his office, his particular creation, his attribute was that he struck people, he bewitched people, he visited people with blisters, festering, pimples, eye pains, watering of the eyes, festering about the eyelashes, lice about the eyes, opacity, filling of the eyes with flesh, withering of the eyes, cataracts, glazing of the eyes.[110]

When sickness befell one of us men, he made a vow to him, he pledged him that he would put on the skin [of the god]: he would don it when the feast day called Tlacaxipeualiztli was celebrated.

All hastened. They pursued one. Many appeared. All went wearing the skin, dripping grease, dripping [blood], glistening, thus terrifying those whom they followed.[111] They fought, joining in battle against the valiant warriors, the chosen ones, the selected, and all who were taking their pleasure, those who became besotted, the buffoons, those who imitated, who pretended to be warriors — the unafraid of death, the jostlers, the perverted warriors. There they exercised their weapons,[112] they skirmished like fighters in war. They ceased [at a place] called Totecco.[113]

Jnic caxtolli vmey, capitulo, ytechpa tlatoa, in teutl: yn itoca, xipe totec.

Anaoatl iteouh: tzapoteca in vel inteuh catca,

yn itequiuh pouja, yn ixcoian ytlachioal, yn ineixcavil: ic temotlaia, ic texoxaia, iehoatl qujtemacaia, in totomonjliztli, papalaniliztli, çaçaoatiliztli, ixcuculiztli, ixchichitinaliztli, ixtenpipixqujliztli, ixtamaçoliciuiztli, ixaiauhpachiuiliztli, ixnacapachiuiliztli, ixoaoaciviztli, ixtotoliciviztli, ixtezcayciuiztli.

Jn aqujn ipam muchioaia, yn, cuculiztli toqujchti, yuicpa monetoltiaia, yujcpa mjtoaia: ynjc onmaqujz yn jieoaio, ynjc itlan aquiz, yn jquac ilhujqujxtililo: motocaiotia, tlacaxipeoaliztli:

tlapainaltiaia, tetocaia, mjequjntin momanaia, muchinti eoaiotiuj, chichiiaoatiuj, chichipicatiuj, tzotzotlantiuj in tetoca, ynjc motlamauhtiliaia: qujnnecaliltiaia, qujnnamjquj in tiiacaoan, tlapepenti, tlatzonanti: yoan in ixqujchti, çan papaqujnj, yn mjhivintia, tlatlamati, moqujchnequj, moqujchnenequj, amjquizmauhque, teca momotlanj, iaotlaveliloque: vncan moieiecoaia, moiaomamachtiaia, yn juh mjcalizque iaopan, vmpa mocacaoaia yn aiac, mjtoaia totecco.

109. Seler (*Tonalamatl of the Aubin Collection*, p. 103) cites Herrera (*Hist. gen.*, Lib. III, cap. 15) to indicate that Xipe enjoyed special honor in the Teotitlan district. A clear discussion of the *"yopimes y tlapanecos"* is given in Sahagún, *op. cit.*, Vol. III, p. 205.

110. Meaning problematical.

111. The corresponding Spanish text describes the scene thus: *"En esta fiesta, hazian como vn juego de cañas: de manera que el vn vando, era de la parte deste dios, o ymagen del dios totec: y estos todos, yuan vestidos de pellejos de hombres que aujan muerto, y desollado, en aquella fiesta. . . . Los del bando contrario, eran los soldados valientes, y osados, y personas velicosas, y esforçadas: que no tenjan en nada, la muerte: osados, atreujdos, que de su voluntad salian, a combatirse, con los otros. Alli los vnos, con los otros, se exercitauã, en el exercicio de la guerra: persegujan los vnos, a los otros: hasta su puesto, y de alli, bolujan huyendo, hasta su proprio puesto."* Cf. also the description in Sahagún, *op. cit.*, Vol. I, p. 144. The game of cañas in the *Enciclopedia Universal Ilustrada*, Vol. II, pp. 299–300, is described as *"Antigua fiesta, juego ó ejercicio caballeresco en que tomaban parte dos bandos ó cuadrillas corriendo á caballo, caracoleando gallardamente y arrojándose cañas de las que se resguardaban con la adarga."* A Moorish exercise, in Medieval times adopted also by the Spaniards, it was reserved to the nobility. It took the form of a picturesque war-game requiring considerable skill in horsemanship and spear-throwing.

112. *Moieiecoaia*: the *Real Palacio MS* has *moeeçouaya* — they covered themselves with blood.

113. For *ayac*, Seler (*Einige Kapitel*, p. 20) suggests *oncan* and translates the passage: *"Man hörte auf an dem sogenannten Totecco (Tempel Xipes)."*

And the young men garbed like Xipe totec, wearing human skins,[114] then went everywhere from house to house. They begged. They were placed on seats made of sapota leaves; they provided them with necklaces formed of maize ears; they placed garlands of flowers on their shoulders; they placed crowns of flowers upon their heads. They gave them to drink.

And if any woman had blisters, or[115] an eye sickness, she said:

"Let me make an offering to Totec, when it is [the feast day] of Tlacaxipeualiztli."

His array [was thus]: he had the quail-painting on his face.[116] Rubber divided his lips in two parts. His *yopi*-crown[117] with forked ends was placed upright. He wore a human skin, the skin of a captive. He had a wig of loose feathers, golden ear plugs, a sapota-leaf skirt. He had bells. His shield had red circles. His rattle stick[118] was in his hand.

Auh yn totecti njman ie ic noujan, tepan cacalaquj, no tlatlaeoa: tzapoicpalpan tlalilo, qujmocholcuzcatia, qujnxochineapanaltia, qujmicpacxochitia, qujntlaoantia.

Auh intla aca cioatl, totomonja, ixcocoieia: qujtoa,

ma njctlamaniliz, in totec, iquac tlacaxipeoaliztli.

Jn inechichioal, mizcolnechimale, tenmaxaltic vltica, yiopitzon contlaliticac maxaliuhquj, conmaqujticac tlacaieoatl, yieoaio malli, tzonchaiaoale, teucujtlanacoche, tzapocueie, tzitzile, ichimal tlauhtevilacachiuhquj, chicaoaztli yn jmac icac.

114. Cf. Sahagún, *op. cit.*, Vol. I, p. 143: *"Todos los pellejos de los desollados se vestían muchos mancebos, a los cuales llamaban* Tototecti." Tototecti is defined as *"los muertos a honra del dios Totec."*

115. The *Real Palacio MS* adds *anoço.*

116. *Real Palacio MS*: *mizçolnechiuale.*

117. Seler (*Gesammelte Abhandlungen*, Vol. II, p. 466) translates *yopi* as "the red people" (Tlapaneca), and gives two illustrations to indicate that they wore pointed caps.

118. "The word *chicauaztli* means 'wherewith anything is made strong.' Word and symbol obviously refer to the strengthening of the reproductive function, to fertilizing. Hence we also saw the *chicauaztli* with the first sign projecting between the human couples in sexual union" (Seler: *Tonalamatl of the Aubin Collection*, p. 100).

Nineteenth Chapter, which telleth of the god named Yiacatecutli (Lord of the Vanguard).[119]

He was the god of the merchants. Greatly they esteemed him. They arrayed in paper their staves, their stout traveling staves[120] with which they journeyed, with which they traveled. Wheresoever they would sleep, there they set them up; before them they did penances, drew blood, offered incense to render service to their god Yiacatecutli, in order to win, to implore his favor.[121]

All manner of places they came to and entered. And hence they were named "the merchants who lead." They took their name from their god, Yiacatecutli.

These vanguard merchants[122] went into the coast lands,[123] looking well for whatsoever goods they could deal in. They went traversing, encircling the coast lands.

They traveled exhausted by the heat and the winds; they traveled exhausted; they went exhausted; they went sighing, walking wearily, in great affliction. Their foreheads burned; the sun's heat held them; they went exposed to its rays.

Jnic caxtolli vnnauj capitulo, ytechpa tlatoa, in teutl: yn jtoca yiacatecutli.

Puchteca inteuh catca: cenca qujmaviztiliaia, qujtlaquentiaia amatica: yn jntopil, ymotlatopil, yn inenemja, yn jmotlatocaia, in cãpa cuchizque, vncan qujtilquetza, ixpan tlamaceoa, mjço, qujcopaltemjlia, ynjc qujtlauhtia yn jnteouh yiacatecutli, ynjc qujtlanjlia, ynjc qujmatataqujlia, yteicneliliz:

noujan acitinemj, calactinemj. Auh ic moteneoa, puchteca yiaque: itech canque, yn itoca inteuh, yiacatecutli:

Oztomeca, anaoac calaqujnj, vel qujtemotinemj, in tlein qujmonanauhtizque, anaoatl qujxaqualotinemj, anaoatl qujlacatzotinemj,

tonalciiauhtinemj, heecaciuhtinemj, mociauhpouhtinemj, mociauhpouhtiuj, elciciuhtiuj, mociauhquetztiuj, ymellelacitiuh, ymjxqua tlatlatiuh, intonal qujmacujtiuj, intonalomjuh ietiuh:

---

119. *"'Yacatecuhtli' no es un nombre propio, sino un nombre de oficio. 'El señor de los que se van.'* Yahqui *es el que se va, el que sale, por el motivo que fuere. En formación de palabras, conforme a las normas del náhuatl, la final*—qui, —que, (*pl*) *tiene que convertirse en* —ca. *No hay duda en esta composición gramatical. Este numen es, por consiguiente, el patrón de los viajeros, por lo cual era el dios propio de los pochtecas, oztomecas, o sea los traficantes a tierras lejanas, que fuera del oficio de comerciantes tenían el de espías y el de avanzadas de conquista"* (Garibay, *Veinte Himnos Sacros de los Nahuas*, p. 204).

120. The corresponding Spanish text states: "*. . . era una caña maziza, que ellos llaman vtlatl. Y tambien usan de otra manera de baculo, que es vna caña negra liujana, maziza: sin ñudo ninguno: que es como junco, de los que se usan en españa."* Clark, in *Codex Mendoza* (James Cooper Clark, ed. and tr.; London: Waterlow and Sons, 1938), Vol. II, p. 106, translates as bamboo (*Bambusa* sp.).

121. Torquemada (*op. cit.*, pp. 57–8) says they gathered the staves all together, girt with a ribbon, worshipping the staves as well as the god.

122. In *Gesammelte Abhandlungen*, Vol. II, p. 1104, Seler states: *"Yacatecutli (der 'Herr der Nase') oder Iyacatecutli (der 'Herr der Weggegangenen') war der Gott der Karawanenführer der* oztomeca anauac calaquini *der reisenden Kaufleute, die die grossen Handelsexpeditionen nach der Tierra caliente leiteten und ausführten."* Sahagún (*op. cit.*, Vol. III, p. 236) refers to the town of Oztotlan in Anahuac as one of the towns famous for the *xiuhtototl*.

123. Anahuac, in addition to designating the valley of Mexico, especially around the lake, refers also to the area in southern Mexico, essentially tropical, which borders the sea coast. In the Spanish version of this chapter, Sahagún defines the area as *"todas las poblaciones, que estan ribera de la mar."* In Book III, Chap. XII, Sahagún states *"Fuéronse hasta* Anáhuac, *que dista más de cien leguas"* (from Tula). Also, *"Entraban en la provincia de Anáhuac, no todos, sino aquellos que iban de parte del señor de México con quien estaban aliados y confederados . . . iban todos juntos hasta el pueblo de* Tochtepec. *En ese pueblo se dividían, unos iban a* Anáhuac Ayotlan; *otros iban a* Anáhuac Xicalanco" (Sahagún, *op. cit.*, Vol. III, p. 28).

They went encountering the deserts; they climbed up and down the gorges, the mountains. They exerted all the strength of their elbows, of their knees to hurry, to go here and there.

ixtlaoatl qujnamjctinemj, atlauhtli, tepetl, qujtemouja, qujtlecauja, ixqujch caana: inmolicpi, intetepon ic tlatlacça, ic moquequetza:

Greatly were they wearied, much did they suffer to seek out the precious green stones, emerald-green jade,[124] fine turquoise,[125] amber, gold; [and] all manner of feathers: the long tail feathers of the resplendent trogon,[126] its red breast feathers,[127] those of the roseate spoonbill,[128] the lovely cotinga,[129] the yellow headed parrot,[130] the troupial,[131] the eagle;[132] and the skins of fierce animals, rugs of ocelot skins, and gourd bowls, incense bowls, tortoise-shell cups, spoons for stirring cacao, stoppers for jars.

vel qujciiavj vel qujhiiouja, ynic qujtemoa in chalchiujtl, in quetzalitztli, in teuxiujtl, yn apoçonalli, in teucujtlatl: in nepapan ihujtl, in quetzalli, in tzinjtzcan, in tlauhquechol, xiuhtototl, in toztli, çaqua: quauhtli, in tequaneoatl, yn ocelupetlatl. Auh in tecomatl, in poctecomatl, in aiutectli, in aquaujtl, yn atzaccaiutl:

In case they were besieged,[133] enclosed, in enemy lands, living among others, having penetrated well within, they became like their enemies. In their array, their hairdress, their speech,[134] they imitated the natives.

intlanel iautitlan, in tzacuj, in tzacutica, tetlan onnemj, vel calaquj, motlacacuepa in nechichioaliztica, in nexintica, in tlatoltica qujntlaehecalhuja in chaneque.

And if they came to an evil pass, if they were discovered, then [the foe] slew them in ambush; they served them up with chili sauce.[135] [But if] anyone — perhaps one, perhaps two — escaped from enemy hands, he went to inform Moctezuma, wherefore he then gave him, he let him insert his amber lip plug. Thereby he did him honor, he singled him out as a valiant warrior. Thus he made him a man of consequence.

Auh intla otlaneçomaltique, intla oittoque: vncan qujnpoiomjctia, qujnchillatilia: ça aca, aço ce, aço vme, yn oc nẽ tematitlanpa qujça, iehoatl qujoalnonotzaia in motecuçuma: ic vncan qujmaca, caqujlia, yapoçonaltenteuh, yc qujmaviziotia, ic qujnezcaiotia, in tiiacauh, vncan ic oqujchtia.

And when they reached their homes, when they had accomplished their return, their homeward jour-

Auh yn jquac oalacia, ynchan: yn jmiloch, ynnecuepal oqujchiuhque, yn otlaltechacico, yn otlaltech-

124. Cf. William F. Foshag: "Mineralogical Studies in Guatemalan Jade," *Smithsonian Miscellaneous Collections*, Vol. 135, No. 5 (Washington: Smithsonian Institution, 1957), p. 8.

125. "Teoxíhuitl, *quiere decir turquesa de los dioses . . . es turquesa fina, y sin ninguna mácula y muy lucida*" (Sahagún, *op. cit.*, Vol. III, p. 334).

126. "*Las plumas que cría en la cola se llaman* quezalli (*y*) *son muy verdes y resplandecientes, son anchas, como unas hojas de espadaña dobléganse cuando las toca el aire* (*y*) *resplandecen muy hermosamente*" (*ibid.*, p. 234).

127. "*El tocado que tiene en la cabeza esta ave* [quetzaltototl] *es muy hermosa y resplandeciente, llaman a estas plumas* tzinitzcan; *tiene esta ave el cuello y el pecho colorado y resplandeciente; es preciosa esta pluma y llámanla* tzinitzcan" (*loc. cit.*). There also is a bird by that name: "*Hay una ave en esta tierra que se llama* tzinitzcan . . . *las plumas preciosas que tiene críalas en el pecho y en los sobacos, y debajo de las alas; son la mitad prietas y la mitad verdes resplandecientes*" (*ibid.*, p. 235).

128. *Tlauhquechol: Ajaia ajaja* (Linnaeus), in Friedmann *et al.*, *op. cit.*, Pt. I, p. 35.

129. Cf. note No. 8.

130. *Toztli*: adult yellow-headed parrot, *Amazona ochrocephala* (Gmelin), in Friedmann *et al.*, Pt. I, p. 131.

131. *Çaqua (çaquan): Gymnostinops montezuma* (Lesson), in Friedmann *et al.*, Pt. II, p. 276.

132. *Quauhtli: Aquila chrysaëtus*, according to Sahagún (Garibay ed.), Vol. IV, p. 330.

133. *Tzacuj: tzaccã* in *Real Palacio MS.*

134. Cf. Torquemada (*op. cit.*, p. 57); Yacacoliuhqui "*propiamente representa persona, que tiene viveça, ò habilidad, para mofar graciosamente, ò engañar, y es sabio, y sagáz (que es propria condicion de Mercaderes). . . .*"

135. Cf. Seler (*Einige Kapitel*, p. 22), citing *Hist. Reyn. Colh. Mex.*, Vol. II, 83.

ney,[136] when they had come to approach their homeland, when they had trodden the earthen mounds, they summoned all, the merchants, the principal men, in order to appear publicly.

pachiuhque: ixqujch tlacatl qujnotza, in puchteca: yoan in tlatoque, ic moteittitiaia:

It was called "the washing of the feet."[137] They paid great honor to the cane, to the walking staff, of Yiacatecutli. Somewhere in [a temple of] the *calpulli*[138] they set it upright; at the first they offered it an offering. When they feasted others, and even if they did not summon people to a banquet, they always offered it an offering when[139] they ate.

mjtoa, mocxipaca, cenca qujmaviztiliaia yn itopil, yn jtlacçaia yiacatecutli: cana in calpulco qujquetzaia: achto qujtlamanjlia, yn jquac tetlaqualtia: yoan intlacanelmo tecoanotza, qujtlamanjlia in çan muchipa yn jtlaquaia.

And if someone were to bathe [a slave] ceremonially, the one whom he ceremonially bathed represented his god Yiacatecutli; or else one of all of them whom they worshipped — Chiconquiauitl, or Chalmecaciuatl, Acxomocuil, and Nacxitl, Cochimetl,[140] Yacapitzauac.[141] No one determined, [for] it was of one's own free will, whether he should bathe one or two men.

Auh intla aca tealtiz, iehoatl caltiaia, qujxeoaia in jteouh yiacatecutli: anoço ceme iehoantin yn mocheoaia, in qujnmoteutiaia in chiconqujaujtl, anoço chalmecacioatl, yoan acxomucujl, yoan nacxitl, cochimetl, iacapitzaoac, aiac qujiocuja, yiollotlama, yn aço ce, anoço vme, caaltiz tlacatl:

They bought them there at the slave market at Atzcaputzalco; they sorted and arranged them, turning them around many times, examining them, buying the good ones — those of good bodies, without blemish, the best men, in good health, sick in no degree, who were marked by no marks on the body.

vmpa concovaia yn tlacanecujloca azcaputzalco: motlahtlatilia, motlapapatilia, qujncuecuepa, qujmjhitta, yn qualtin qujncoazque, yn acan quenamjque, in tlacaiecti, in tlacamelaoaque, yn acan cucuxque, yn atle intlaciuh ca:

Such as these they slew on the feast day, Panquetzaliztli, when the feast day of Uitzilopochtli was celebrated.

ynjc iehoan qujnmictizque, yn ipan panquetzaliztli: yn vncan ilhujqujxtililoia vitzilubuchtli:

Thereupon they arrayed them; they gave them, they placed upon them array like that of Yiacatecutli.

yquac qujnchichioaia, qujntlamamaca, intech qujtlalia yn juhquj ynechichioal yiacatecutli.

And before they slew them, they first exhibited them before the people. It was said that they showed them; thus they made public that they would ceremonially bathe slaves.

Auh yn aiamo qujnmjctia, achtopa qujnteittitiaia: mjtoa qujmjxnextia, ic qujtemachitia in tealtizque:

At this time they gave gifts and had a feast.

iquac tetlauhtia, tetlaqualtia.

And their bathed ones they set up in a good place, all in costly mantles, which they placed upon them.

Auh yn j̃tlaaltilhoan, ieccan, qujnquetza: much tlaçotilmatli, yn jntech qujntlalilia: ipã mjtotiaia in

136. *Otlaltechpachiuhque: otlatelpachiuhque* in the *Real Palacio MS.* Seler's translation (*Einige Kapitel,* p. 22) is *"ihr fuss die Erdaufschüttungen (der heimatlichen Tempel und Paläste) wieder betreten hatte."*

137. Book IX of the *Historia general* deals almost entirely with the activities of the merchants. Chapter VI, entitled *De la ceremonia que se hacia a los mercaderes cuando llegaban a su casa, que se llama lavatorio de pies,* mentions washing mouth and hands.

138. Sahagún defines *calpulli* as *"yglesia del barrjo, o perrocha"* (corresponding Spanish text). For recent studies on the *calpulli* see Alfonso Caso: "Land Tenure among the Ancient Mexicans," *American Anthropologist,* Vol. 65, No. 4 (Aug., 1963), pp. 863–878, and Pedro Carrasco: "El Barrio y la Regulación del Matrimonio en un Pueblo del Valle de México en el Siglo XVI," *Revista Mexicana de Estudios Antropológicos,* Vol. 17 (1961), pp. 7–24.

139. After *muchipa, Real Palacio MS* adds *yn iquac.*

140. *Cochimetl*: in *Real Palacio MS, cocochimetl.*

141. According to the Spanish version, they were four brothers and a sister of Yiacatecutli. Seler (*Gesammelte Abhandlungen,* Vol. II, p. 1106) recognizes Cochimetl and Yacapitzauac as synonyms for Yiacatecutli; Chiconquiauitl or Chalmecaciuatl is an earth and water goddess; Acxomocuil is Tezcatlipoca; Nacxitl is Quetzalcoatl.

In these they danced upon the rooftops or went singing in the market place. They ended their song mocking death.

tlapanco, anoço tianquizco: cujcatinemj, tlatlahtlamj yn jncujc, ynjc momiquizquequeloa.

And if any were noted who were very subtle, among the bathed ones — one skilled in songs, one who was ingenious, who was intelligent and able — the noblemen set him aside and put another in his place.

Auh intla aca oittoc, in cenca mjmati tlaaltilli, yn cujcamatinj, in iolizmatquj, yn jxe, yn iollo: qujqujxtiaia in pipilti, ipan tlacaquetzaia:

Likewise, if a woman could embroider, or if she prepared food well, or made good cacao — from her hand good food, good drink came — [or if she were] a clear speaker, she also was set aside. The nobles took [women like her] as wives.

no iuhquj, intla cioatl, intla tlamachiuhquj, anoço vellaqualchioa, vel achioa, in qualli yiauh, in qualli intlaqual ymac quiça; vellatolmelaoac: no qujxtiloia, qujnmotlacacioaoatiaia in pipilti.

His array [was thus][142] put on: pyrites were on his face. In the form of a column was his headdress with tufts of quetzal feathers. He wore golden ear plugs. A blue netted cloth was his cape. He had a costly breech-clout. He had bells and shells. He wore princely sandals. His shield was of quetzal feathers in a fretted design. His traveling staff was in his hand; he had a stout cane staff.

Jn jnechichioal motlatlatlali, mixapetzvi, ytemjlo, ixquatzo, ixquatzone, quetzallalpile, teucujtlanacoche, xiuhtlalpilli yn jtilma, tlaçomaxtle, tzitzile, oiooale, teccaque, quetzalxicalcoliuhquj yn jchimal, ytlacçaia ymac onoc, otlatopile.

142. After *jnechichioal, Real Palacio MS* adds *ynic mochichiua.*

Twentieth Chapter, which telleth of the god whose name was Napa tecutli (Lord of the Four Directions).

Jnic cempoalli capitulo, ytechpa tlatoa yn teutl yn jtoca catca Napa tecutli.

It is said that he also belonged among the Tlalocs. His was a special place, a *calpulli.* The mat-makers worshipped him, and those who made round reed mats [and] coarse reed mats.[143] It was attributed to him, so they said, that he first taught them, showed them the making of reed mats, the making of reed seats. He was possessor, master, owner, inventor, founder, beginner [of mat making]. And thus they said that he caused to sprout, to grow, the reeds, the slender reeds, the broad reeds, the cylindrical reeds, the white reeds, the reed stalks, the spikes, the triangular reeds, the thin ones.

Juh mjtoa, ca no intech pouj yn tlaloque: iehoan ymjxcoian, incatjan, in calpolloc, qujmoteutiaia in petlachiuhque: yoan tolcuechiuhque, in tlacuechjuhque, ytech mopoaia: iuh qujtoaia, ca iehoatl achto qujnmachti, qujmittiti, in petlachioaliztli, yn icpalchioaliztli: iehoatl axcaoa cococaoaia, tlatqujoa, tlanextile, tlatzintile, tlapeoaltile. Joan iuh qujtoaia ca iehoatl qujxoaltia, qujqujxtia, in toli, in tolpitzaoac, in tolpatlactli, in tolmjmjlli, aztapili, in tolqujiutl, in tolcaputl, yn jtztoli, xomali:

And when it was his feast day, it is said, he washed men, he bathed men,[144] he shook, he sprinkled the dew upon them. Greatly was he importuned.

yoan yn jquac ilhujuhqujçaia, iuh mjtoa, tepapaca, tealtia, tepan qujtzetzeloa, tepan qujpixoa, yn aoachtli, cenca tlaihtlanjliloia.

And another person represented him, a slave, whom they sacrificed during the year. They arrayed him [like the god], and in his hand went resting a green gourd vessel, in which was water. With a willow[145] he sprinkled people.[146]

Auh no ce tlacatl, ipan qujxeoaia, tlacotli, in qujmictiaia cexiuhtica: qujchichioaia, ymac mantinenca, xoxoujc, xoxouhquj xicalli: vncan ietinemj atl, vexotica ic teatzelhvia.

And when it was not his feast day, in the intervening time, still another represented him; they arrayed him. When one of the mat-makers desired that there should be a dance at his home, that he should entrust himself to the god, the elders of the *calpulli* escorted [the representative of the god] there. He went sprinkling the people with water, with dew.[147] It was thus as if they prayed [to the god] that he would show them mercy. And it was as if[148] one's debt were paid to the degree that one's goods, one's possessions, were at hand.

Auh yn jquac amo ilhujuh, yn çan nenmajan: oc no ce qujxiptlaiotiaia, qujchichioaia: yn jquac tla aca, petlachiuhquj qujnequj ychan qujtotiz, qujnepieltiz: vmpa qujvicaia, in calpuleque, teatzelhujtiuh, teaoachvitiuh, iuhqujn ic qujtlanjliaia, ynjc qujmicneliz. Yoan iuhqujn yvic mocujtlaxculixtlaoaia: yn açaca ie vnca itlatquj, yaxca:

---

143. Corresponding Spanish text says, *"hazen cañizos de juncias; que llaman tolcuextli."*

144. *Tealtia*: in *Real Palacio MS, teaaltia.*

145. The corresponding Spanish text specifies *"vn ramo de salze"* (*sauce*).

146. *Teatzelhvia*: in *Real Palacio MS, teaatzeluıa.*

147. *Teaoachvitiuh*: *teauachitiuh* in *ibid.*

148. After *iuhqujn, ic* is added in *ibid.*

He said: "May I eat not in vain, may I consume not in vain, may I use not for myself alone that which hath benefited me. May there be eating, may there be drinking, may there be consumption of food; thereupon may our god Napa tecutli dance. May I to some degree conduct myself well, soon sleep, soon awaken. [The god] knoweth if he will give anything to me, if he willeth that anything be given."

qujtoaia, macamo njcnenqua, macamo njcnenpolo, macamo njcnixcauj, yn nocneliloca: ma onqualo, ma onjoa, ma onpopoliuj, ma ic onmjtoti in toteouh napa tecutli: ma çaquen njnonemjtiz, yn aciuhquj njcochiz, aciuhquj njneoaz, iehe qujmati, yn açoc itla, nechmomaqujliz, qujmomacaviliz:

Then he covered the face of the one who had become the representative with a large cotton mantle, whereupon he departed from [the mat-maker's] house. And then [the mat-maker] feasted all his kinsmen.

ic quixquentiaia ce quachtli, yn ixiptla muchioaia, ic oalquiça yn ichan: auh ic muchi tlacatl, tlatlaquaia yn joaniolque.

And the representative [of the god] was guarded there in the temple of the *calpulli.* The mat-makers greatly honored and cared for him. Always they spread out mats and set up seats; they shook things out, they swept clean, they removed rubbish, they laid fires. Always they provided incense. The floor lay cleanly swept; it extended cleanly swept; not a particle of rubbish lay about.

Auh yn jcalpulco in vmpa pialoia yxiptla, cenca tlamauiztiliaia, tlâceliaia, in petlachiuhque, muchipa petlateteca, icpalteteca, tlatzetzeloa, tlachpana, tlacuicuj, tletlalia, muchipa copaltema, tlatetzcaliuhtoc tlatetzcaliuhtimanj, atle vetztoc çe tlaçolli.

And thus was he arrayed: he was anointed with black; his face was covered with soot; it was blackened; his face was [spotted] with [a paste of] amaranth seed dough. He wore a paper crown. His cue at the nape of his neck was of paper. He wore a paper breech-clout. He had bells. He had white sandals. He bore the shield with water-lily flowers. He had a stout reed staff.[149]

Auh yujn yn muchichioaia, motliloçac, mjxtlilpopotz, mixtlilhuj, mjchchiaujticac, amacale, yiamacuexpal, amamaxtle, tzitzile, iztaccaque, atlacueçonanchimale, aztapiltopile.

149. The last two words read: *atlacueçonachimale oztopiltopile* in *ibid.*

Twenty-first Chapter, which telleth of those called the Tepictoton (Little Molded Ones), who belonged among the Tlalocs.

[The Tepictoton] also belonged among, were reckoned among the Tlalocs.

They were called Tepictoton[150] because they just formed them: they made them in the image of the mountains,[151] of whatsoever mountains.

And he who was palsied, cramped, stiffened, paralyzed, or he who was threatened with drowning, when the wind rose over the water, would then vow that he would fashion images; that he would mold representations of Quetzalcoatl, Chalchiuitl ycue, Tlaloc, Popocatepetl, Iztac tepetl, Poiauhtecatl,[152] and any other mountain of which they would choose to make representations.

And he who formed mountains made their image only of amaranth seed dough,[153] made in human form, made to look like men. He gave them teeth of gourd seeds; he provided them with eyes of fat black beans. Whatsoever their array, when they represented them, when they formed them, they arrayed them in the same manner.

And they made papers; they spotted, spattered them with liquid rubber;[154] they laid these over them as mantles. And some of these papers, spattered, spotted with liquid rubber, they hung on a cord, bound together on a cord, fastened together, so that they were held in a row before the small molded ones. They extended rustling, quivering, flying in the breeze. At both ends canes of fat, round reeds were set in the ground, supported by the ground. On these were held the rubber-spotted papers.

Jnic cempoalli vce capitulo ytechpa tlatoa yn itoca tepictoton: yn jnoan pouja tlaloque.

No ynoan pouj, intech tlamjloia yn tlaloque:

ynjc mjtoaia tepicto, çan qujmonpiqujia, qujmixiptlaiotiaia, in tetepe, in çaço catle tepetl.

Auh yn aqujn coaciujia, oaoapaoaia, quaquauhtia, cocototzauja: anoço yn aqujn atlan miquiznequj, ehecatl ipan moquetza atla: vncan monetoltiaia ynjc tepiquiz, in qujnpiquiz: quetzalcoatl, in chalchivitl ycue, in tlaloc: popucatepetl, iztac tepetl, poiauhtecatl: yoan in çaço quezqujtetl tepetl in qujnteneoaz in qujpiquiz.

Auh in qujnpiquja, in qujmixiptlatiaia in tetepe, çan tzoalli, qujntlacatlaliaia, qujntlacatlachieltiaia, tlacatlachixticatca: qujntlantiaia aiooachtli, auh in qujmjxtelolotiaia aiecutli: in quenamj yntlatquj in qujmixiptlatiaia, in qujnpiqujia çan no iuhquj ynjc qujnchichioaia.

Auh yoan qujchioaia, amateteujtl, colchachapatzaia, colchipiniaia, qujnquequentiaia: auh in cequj amatetevitl, tlaolchipinjlli, tlaolchachapatzalli, mecatitech qujpipiloaia, mecatitech qujnenetechilpiaia, qujnenetechçaloaia, ymjxpan antoc, ic itzacutoque in tepicme: hiçanacatoc papapatlacatoc, papatlantoc, oztopilquaujtl, necoc, nenecoc, necoccampa tlatlalacticac, tetzotzonticac, yn itech antoc teteujtl.

---

150. *Tepictotõ* in *ibid.*

151. *Q'mixiptlatiaya* in *ibid.*

152. Gods of the air, of water, and of rain (cf. corresponding Spanish text). Popocatepetl and Iztac tepetl (Iztac ciuatl) are mountain-peaks in the Valley of Mexico; Poiauhtecatl is Mt. Orizaba.

153. Made of dough (*vna massa*) in the Spanish column; Seler renders it *zerquetschten Samen des Stachelmohns* (*Einige Kapitel*, p. 27).

154. ". . . *unos papeles llenos de gotas de* ulli, *a los cuales papeles llamaban* amateteuitl" (Sahagún, Garibay ed., Vol. I, p. 140).

And green spotted gourds, split in two and cored, rested before [the Tepicme]; these served as greenstone bowls; there was wine therein, wine rested in each one.

Auh tzilacaiutli, tlaixtlapantli, tlaittitatactli: ymixpan mamanca, chalchiuhxicalli ipam poujia, vctli vnca ca, vctli ic mamanca.

And it was the office of the priests alone, who were experienced, to array, to set [the Tepicme] in place; no one else took it upon himself[155] to array them in the houses.

Auh çan iehoan in tlamacazque, yn jntequiuh, in machiceque catca, yn qujnchichioaia, in qujntlaliaia: aiac çan moiocuiaia, in calla in qujnchichioaia.

And on the fifth [day], when they invited the priests, it was said, they caused them to forget.

Auh macujltica in qujntlalhujaia, mjtoa: qujnmolcaoaltiaia in tlamacazque:

When the Tepicme were completed, thereupon they held a vigil for them; they sang for them all during the night. Four times they made offerings to them; they gave them, they set before them round tamales. The priests who provided the Tepicme with song, they also gave offerings four times during the night. And they played flutes for [the Tepicme], they whistled with their fingers, they made music for them with shells, and with flutes, with fifes. The youths, the fun-makers, the jesters,[156] the besotted, the entertainers, the joy-makers played the flutes. They also were offered food.

yn oiecauhque tepicme, njman ie ic qujntoçaviia, qujncujcatia: in ceiooal napa in qujntlamanjlia, tamalololli in qujnmacaia, qujmanaia ymjxpã, in tlamacazque, in tepiccujca: no napa in qujntlamacaia ceiooal, yoan qujntlapichiliaia, qujnmaquiqujxiliaia, tecuciztli in qujnpichiliaia, yoan vilacapitztli, cocoujlotl, vilacapitzoaia, çan telpopochti, papaqujnj, haavienj, mihivintianj, tececemeltianj, ceceleque, no tlamacoia.

And when it had dawned then they slew the Tepicme; they beheaded them, twisted their heads off, wrung their necks. Then they gathered together,[157] collected together the amaranth seed dough formed into figures; they carried it to the priests' house, where the priests dwelt. And he who fashioned the Tepicme thereupon returned to his guests, his invited ones, where he tarried, where they remained.

Auh yn otlatvic njman qujnmictia yn tepicme, qujnquechcotona, qujnquechcuj, qujnquechilacatzoa, çatepan qujncemololoa, concẽcuj, in tepictzoalli, qujtquj yn calmecac yn vmpa onoque, tlamacazque. Auh in tepiqujnj, njman ie yc calaqujh yn itlacoanotzalhoan, yn jcooaoan, vncan mopia, mopixtoque:

And in the evening, when the sun set, then there was drinking of wine. The old men sat drinking wine[158]—those already advanced in age, the well-matured, the gray-headed, the white-haired, the old women, those whose privilege it was to drink wine.

auh in ie iooatiuh, in ie tevtlac niman ie ic tlaoana, motlaoancatlalia in veuetlaca, yn ie chicaoaque, yn otlachicalhujque, in ie quaiztaque, in ie tzoniztaque, yoan ilamatlaca yn jlamatque: iehoan vel innemac catca, in vctli in quizque.

And when they had drunk their fill, thereupon all went to their houses, dispersed and scattered.

Auh in otlaivintic, niman ie ic viujloa, cecenmanoia, xixitinjoa:

One went weeping; another went as a brave warrior, dancing, boasting; another went shouting at the people.

yn aca mochoqujlitiuh, yn aca moqujchitotiuh, mjtotitiuh, momamantiuh: yn aca tetzatzilitiuh.

And the wine-makers were first made to forget. They also dwelt there. The making [of the wine] was their office. It was explained that for four days they should fast and abstain during their work, lest

Auh in vctlali, achto molcaoaltiloia: çan no onnenca yn itequjuh, yn jchiujl: tlacaqujtiloia, navilhujtl moçaoaia, qujneçaujliaia yn itequjuh, ynic amo xocoiaz: vel mopiaia, vel motlacaoaltiaia, amo cioaco-

155. *Moiocuiaia: moyocuaya* in *Real Palacio MS.*

156. *Haavienj: haaviani* in *ibid.*

157. *Qujncemololoa: cõcemololoa* in *ibid.*

158. *Motlaoancatlalia: motlauãcatlaliya* in *ibid.*

[the wine] sour. They guarded themselves well; they practised strict abstinence; no man might lie with a woman; if a woman, she might not lie with a man. None might sample the wine and the maguey syrup as it was being prepared. One might not even dip one's finger into it; it was respected, treated delicately, until the wine was tapped.[159]

And of him who secretly tasted it, who in secret drank some, even tasting only a little, it was said that his mouth would become twisted, it would stretch to one side;[160] to one side his mouth would shift; it would be drawn over.

And if one were lame in one hand, [if] his arm quivered, his leg quivered, a hand became misshapen, a foot became misshapen, his foot shook,[161] his eyes trembled, his lips quivered, his lips trembled, if he were possessed, it was said, the green mountain gods had become angered by him.

And when it dawned, thereupon took place the distribution of the leftovers. At the distribution, only the relatives, the people of the household — his family, they of the same parentage, of the same womb, those of the same lineage [took part]. It was called the distribution of the leftovers, when was consumed, used up,[162] as much food and drink as remained, and of that which still remained of the dregs in the vessel, of wine, of fermentative agent,[163] of fruit wine, of sleep-producing wine.

And he who fashioned the Tepicme, who had made the Tepicme, if he had the gout, as was said above, would thereby become whole. And he who might have drowned therefore did not die. This one therefore formed the Tepicme; thus he paid his debt; thus he fulfilled his vow.

And all their adornment — their clothing, their paper shoulder-sashes, their stout reed staves, their lightning sticks, their cloud-bundles,[164] and their green-stone bowls and their dishes, the little sauce bowls, the little wooden bowls, the clay cups, all these they left at Tepetzinco: they threw them into the water, off shore, at a place called Pantitlan.

chia, amo oqujchcochia, intla cioatl: çan niman aiac vel ontlapaloaia yn vctli, yoan in necutli, ynic muchioaia: aiac inmanel imapil, conaqujaia, vel ymacaxoa, vel malhujloia, yn ixqujchica, moiacaxapotlaz yn vctli.

Auh yn aqujn, ichtaca tlapaloaia, yn tlachtaca yia inmanel çan tepiton oconpalo: iuh mjtoaia tennecujlivia tepantiliviia, avic momamana avic xoqujvi yn ite:

yoan in aca matzicoliujia, yma qujcuecuetza, icxi quicuecuetza, macopichauj, icxicopichauj, icxicuecuechca, yhixatotoco, tenpapatlaca, tenviviioca, itech qujneoa: mjtoa, oqujtlavelique in xoxouhque tepicme.

Auh yn otlathujc, njman ie ic apeoalo: yn apeoa çan iehoan, yn ioaniolque, in vel icalloc, in centlaca, cemeoa, in vel icujtlaxcolloc, yn vel imecaioc: moteneoa apeoalo, iquac cempoliuja tlatlamj, in quexqujch mocaoaia, in atl, in tlaqualli: yoan in oc quexqujch omocauh xaiocomjc in vctli, in aiuctli, in tlachioalvctli, in iztac vctli, in cochvctli.

Auh yn tepiqujnj, in tepicquj: intla coacivi, yn juh omjto tlacpac, ic patiz: yoan yn aqujn atlan miquizquja ynjc amo mjc: iehoatl, ynjc tepiquj, ynjc moxtlaoa, ynjc qujneltilia ynnetol.

Auh yn jxqujch. yn jnnechichioal, yn jntlaquen, yn jmamaneapan, yn jmoztopil, yn jntlapetlanjlquauh, yn jmaiauhcocul: yoan yn jnchalchiuhxical, yoã yn jntlaquaia molcaxtototonti, quauhcaxtototonti, çoqujtecontototonti, muchi vmpa concaoaia tepetzinco: atlan contepeoaia, vmpa anepantla, ytocaiocan pantitlan.

159. Cf. Seler, *op. cit.*, p. 29, citing marginal gloss in *MS Biblioteca del Palacio.* Cf. also explanation in Sahagún, *op. cit.*, Vol. I, p. 63.

160. *Tepantiliviia: Tenpatiliviya* in the *Real Palacio MS.*

161. *Icxicuecuechca: yxcuecuechca* in *ibid.*

162. *Cempoliuja tlatlamj: cenpopoliuiya tlatlatlami* in *ibid.*

163. *Aiuctli: "Ingrediente vegetal, raíz, planta, o madera usado para hacer fermentar el pulque. . . . Conjeturalmente se puede señalar* Mimosa *sp.* Acacia *sp."* (Sahagún, Garibay ed., Vol. IV, p. 324).

164. Alvaro Tezozomoc, *Histoire de Mexique* (H. Ternaux-Compans, tr.; Paris: P. Jannet, 1853), Vol. I, p. 300, describes this as a light flame-colored club: ". . . *on eût dit qu'il en sortait des flammes et des étincelles.*" Seler (*op. cit.*, p. 30) calls it a lightning stick (*Blitzholz*).

Tezcatzoncatl.

Twenty-second Chapter, which telleth of the god Tezcatzoncatl, who belonged among the Centzontotochti (The Four Hundred Rabbits).

He was the wine, in times past considered full of sin. For he hurled people off crags, he strangled people, he drowned people, he killed them. He was an awesome being, one not to be affronted, one not to be abused.

And this Tezcatzoncatl belonged among, was considered with those called the four hundred rabbits, who are the substance of wine — Yiauhtecatl, Acolhua, Tlilhoa, Pantecatl, Izquitecatl, Toltecatl, Papaztac, Tlaltecaioa, Ome Tochtli, Tepoztecatl, Chimalpanecatl, Colhuatzincatl.

And the array of Tezcatzoncatl [was thus]: he had the white heron feather headdress; he had the crescent-shaped nose ornament, the ear plug of paper. He bore a fan of red arara feathers, a radiating necklace. He had the knotted cape with [representations of] scorpions. He carried the wine gods' shield, the obsidian staff, the flint staff. Also he had bells.

End of the Book

Jnic cempoalli vmume capitulo, ytechpa tlatoa in tezcatzoncatl. yn jnoan pouj centzontotochti.

Jehoatl in vctli, ieppa tlatlaculli ipan machoia: ca tetepexiuja, tequechmecanja, teatlauja, temjctia; tetzavittonj, amo pinavilonj, amo chicoittolonj.

Auh ynjn tezcatzoncatl, ynoan pouj, ynoan eoa, yn moteneoa, centzõtotochti, yn vctli innacaio, yn iJauhtecatl, Aculhoa, tlilhoa, pantecatl, Jzqujtecatl, Toltecatl, papaztac, Tlaltecaiooa, vme tuchtli, tepuztecatl, chimalpanecatl, Colhoatzincatl.

Auh yn jnechichioal Tezcatzoncatl, aztatzone, iacametze, amanacoche, cveçalvitoncaoa, chaiaoac cuzque, colotlalpile, vmetuchchimale, itztopile, tecpatopile, no tzitzile.

fin del libro.

APPENDIX

Apendiz
del primero libro

Comiença el apendiz, del primero libro: en que se confuta la ydolotria, arriba puesta: por el testo, de la sagrada escriptura, y buelta en lengua mexicana: declarando, el testo suficientemente.

[Here] beginneth the appendix to Book I, in which the idolatry described above is refuted by means of sacred scriptural texts translated into the Mexican tongue, the texts being sufficiently explained.

Prologue

Ye who are natives in New Spain, ye Mexicans, ye Tlaxcalans, ye Cholulans, ye Michoaca, and all ye who are vassals dwelling in the land of the Indies —

Very great was the darkness and the confusion, the unbelief, the idolatry in which your fathers, your grandfathers, your great-grandfathers left you, as is evident in your ancient picture writings.

Hear and understand well. For now our Lord, God, hath willed, hath accorded, hath sent to you the brightness, the torch, the light to reveal the true God, the Creator Who seeth over all His creation.

And confusion, in which you have lived in all past time, came to you. It hath misled and deluded you. But by means of the brightness, the light, you may attain true faith.

And thus you may accept, you may hear the word of God, here written, which he, your lord, the King of Spain, hath sent to you, as well as God's Vicar, the Holy Father, who dwelleth in Rome.

And for this reason they have caused this to be done, that you may escape the hands of the devils, and that you may attain the Kingdom of Heaven.

The Declaration of God's Word[165]

The people here on earth who know not God are not counted as human; they are only vain, worthless. For if men in their hearts, in their understanding, knew God's creations, from them they would have

Comiença el apendiz, del primero libro: en que se confuta la ydolatria, arriba puesta: por el testo, de la sagrada escriptura, y buelta en lengua mexicana: declarando, el testo suficientemente.

Prologo, mexicano

In amehoantin, in njcan antlaca, in nueua españa: in anmexica, in antlaxcalteca, in ancholulteca, in anmjchoaque, yoan in amjxqujchtin in anmacehoaltin, in njcan annemj in india tlalli ipan:

ca cenca vey tlaiooalli, yoan netlapololtiliztli, yn atlaneltoqujliztli, in tlateutoqujliztli, in jpan oamechcauhtiaque yn amotahoan, yn amoculhoan, yn amachcoculhoan: yn juh neci, in ipã ie uecauh amotlacujlol:

ma vel cenca xiccaqujcan, vel xicacicacaqujcan. Ca in axcan, oqujmonequjlti in totecujo dios, otlacauhquj in jiollotzin, yn oamechoalmjoalili, in tlaujlli, in ocotl, in tlanextli: injc anqujmjximachilizque, in vel nelli dios teiocuianj, in qujmocujtlaujtzinoa, in jxqujch in jtlachioaltzin.

Auh yn netlapololtiliztli, yn jpan annemj yn jxqujch cavitl, vmpa otioallaque: ca iehoatl yn amechiztlacaujaia, amechtlapololtiaia: auh in tlavilli, in tlanextli anqujcnopilhuizque, yn jca vel melaoac tlaneltoqujliztli:

yoan ic vel anqujcuizque, anqujcaquizque, in jtlatoltzin dios, yn njcan icujliuhtica: in vel iehoatl in amotlatocatzin in españa rey, in amechvalmjvalili: no iehoatzin in jxiptlatzin Dios in Sancto padre, in roma moyetztica.

Auh injn ca ipampa oqujmuchivilique, injc inmac anqujçazque in diablosme: ioan ynjc anqujcnopilvizque yn jlvicac tlatocaiotl.

Jmelaoaca in teutlatolli.

Jn tlalticpac tlaca, yn amo qujmiximachilia in dios, ca amo tlaca ipan pouj, ca çan nentlaca, nenquizque: ca intla tlaca yntla vnca iniollo, intla vnca intlacaqujliz: in jtlachioalhoan dios, intech canazquja, intech

165. The non-Aztec text begins here the thirteenth, fourteenth, twelfth, fifteenth, and sixteenth chapters of the *Book of Wisdom*. The Nahuatl text parallels rather than translates the Latin.

derived, they would have grasped, their knowledge of God. Because they esteem and know creatures they should have known that He existeth, that He is the Creator, the Creator of man — God, Who is not seen.

But these did not so; they took not example of God's creations. Thus they should have recognized their gods, their lords as the creatures of God. Only they were in confusion as to God's creatures; they worshipped as gods the fire, the water, the wind, the sun, the moon, the stars. These things they worshipped as gods. They said that by means of them we live; they guide us, they protect us. They support, they carry.

A. These were blind, they were confused, in being idolaters. Greatly they honored God's creatures, as if they enlightened, revealed, and gave comfort to men. And these should not be thus worshipped, because it should only be remembered that He Who is most powerful, in giving light, illumination, comfort, joy, is God, their Creator; He from Whom alone issueth that which illumineth, that which giveth light, that which comforteth; all teaching — He alone, the Creator.

B. And if they had wondered greatly because some of God's creatures are strong, they should have remembered that God, their Creator, is even stronger.

C. God the all-powerful is so completely wise, so greatly enriching, completely glorifying that His creatures appear in Him. For He is very great. He made the world. Very many things made He which were very wonderful, very glorifying.

D. These, the idolaters, excused themselves; they drew away. They said: "We have sought Him for ourselves; we have coveted Him through Whom we live, the Creator. But we have taken Him to be the sun, the moon, the stars, and still other creations, because they are wonderful, highly valued; they give men great comfort, they enrich men. For truly we are not men of strong heart and understanding."

E. These words, with which the idolaters sought to excuse themselves, in no way quieted men's doubts but only angered men. For this reason did they not quiet men's doubts: for those who began idolatry made known, discovered many things — dangerous

qujcuizquja, in jximachocatzin dios; ipampa qujmitta in qujximati in tlachioalti, qujmatizquja ca vmmoetztica, monemjtia in tlachioale, in teiucoianj, yn amo motta in iehoatzin dios.

Auh ynjn ca amo iuhquj qujchiuhque, amo itech omjscujtique, yn jtlachioalhoan dios: ynjc qujmjximachilizquja yn jnteouh, yn jntlatocauh, yn jnteiocuscatzin dios, çan ītech omotlapololtique yn jtlachioalhoan dios: oqujmoteutique in tletl, in atl, in ehecatl, in tonatiuh, in metztli, in cicitlalti; iehoãtin hi, oqujnmoteutique, qujtoque, ca impal tinemj, ca techiacana, techpachoa, ca tlatquj, ca tlamama.

A. Jn iehoantin, y, ca ixpopoiume, motlapololtianj, injc otlateutocaque: ca cenca qujmaujçoque, yn jtlachioalhoan dios, ynjc tlanextia, ynjc pepetlaca, in teiollalia: auh ynjn amo ic qujmoteutizquja: ca çan ic qujlnamjquizquja, ca oc cenca tlapanauja, ynjc cenca tlanextia, pepetlaca, teiollalia, tepapaqujltia, yn jnteiocuxcatzin dios: in çan vel iceltzin itetzinco quiça in pepetlaca, in tlanextia, in jxqujch teiollali, yn jxqujch tetlamachti, vel iehoatzin çan vel izeltzin, tlachioale.

B. Auh intla cenca otlamaujçoque ipampa cequjnti itlachioalhoan dios, cenca chicaoaque: qujlnamjquizquja, ca yn jnteiocuxcatzin dios, oc cenca chicaoacatzintli.

C. Jn jsqujch iueli, in dios, ynjc cenquizca tlamatinj, ynjc cenca tecujltono, cenquizca tetlamachti: ca ytlachioaltzin itech neci: iehica ca cenca vey, cemanaoac oqujmuchiujli, cenca mjec tlamantli, oqujmuchiujli, vel mauiztic, vel tetlamachti.

D. Jnjque hi, tlateutocanjme, momanauja, motzinqujxtia, qujtoa: in tehoanti, ca iehoatzi tictotemulia, in iehoatzin tiqueleuja, yn jpalnemoanj, in teiocujanj: auh ca ytech otitotzotzonato, in tonatiuh, in metztli, in cicitlalti, yoan oc cequj tlachioalti: ipampa ca mauiztique, vellaçoti, cenca teiollalique, vel tetlamachtique: ca nel titlaca amo chicaoac, in toiollo, in totlamachiliz.

E. Jnjn tlatolli, ynjc momanauiznequj tlateutocanjme: ca amo teiolpachiujti, ca çan tequalanj, ipampa amo teiolpachiujti: ca in iehoantin, oquipeoaltique, in tlateutoqujliztli, mjec tlamantli oqujnextique, oqujttaque, in ouj tlatolli: in xiuhtlapoaliztli, in

teachings; they discovered, they made known the year count, the day count, and still other dangerous teachings. But just as they consulted among themselves, just as they deliberated in order to know what hath been said, just so, much better, could they have known, could they have discovered Him through Whom we live, the Creator, if they had deliberated — if they had consulted among themselves.

tonalpoaliztli, yoan in oc cequj ouj tlatolli, oqujttaque, oqujnextique: auh in quenjn omojolnonotzque, in quenjn oqujnemjlique, injc oqujximatque in omoteneuh: çan no iuhquj, oc oalca, ynjc qujximatizquja, qujttazquja, yn jpalnemoanj, in tlachioale, intla vellanemjlianj, intla vel moiolnonotzanj.

F. Unhappy are they, the accursed dead who worshipped as gods carvings of stone, carvings of wood, representations, images, things made of gold or of copper, or who indeed worshipped as gods four-footed animals, creatures which fly, those which live in the waters, or their representations which carpenters or lapidaries carved, or metal-workers molded.

F. Ointlaueliltic, in iehoanti, in tlacamjccapupul, in qujmoteutique, in tetlaxintli, in quaujtl tlaxintli, in teixiptla, in tepatillo: in teucujtlatl, yn anoço tepuztli, ic tlachiuhtli: yn anoço ie oqujmoteutique, in manenemj, yn patlantinemj, in atlan nemj: yn anoço ymjxiptlaoan, in qujnxinque, in quauhxinque, in tetzotzonque, yn anoço in teucujtlapitzque, oqujpitzque.

G. Behold the works of the idolaters which can greatly confuse men, which can terrify men. For if some wood-carver wisheth to make his god, he goeth there into the forest. He felleth a tree. It is good, it is tall and straight. And then he striketh off its branches, he cutteth off its branches. And the bark, the leaves of the tree go there unto his house; there they will be required in order to cook his food. And the tree he cutteth up. He maketh a log, a cylinder of wood. And while it is still a log, well doth he carve it; carefully doth he continue to carve it. He giveth it a head, eyes, a face, a body, hands, feet. And when he hath finished, then against the wall he buildeth a house for it. There he standeth it. And that it may not fall, he holdeth it firmly to the wall's surface with either pegs or iron nails.

G. Jzcatquj, yn jntlachioal yn tlateutocanjme in cenca vel tetlapalolti, in vel teiçauj, ca in aca quauhxinquj qujchioaznequj yn jteouh, vmpa iauh in quauhtla, ce quaujtl qujtlaça, ie in qualli, ie in melaoac: auh njman qujmatlatlaça, qujmatepeoa: auh yn jmama, yn jmatzocul in quaujtl, vmpa iauh yn jchan, vmpa monequiz: ynjc ycuciz, ytlaqual. Auh in quaujtl, qujtequj: cen tlacutl, quauhtemjmjlli, qujchioa: auh yn oc cen tlacutl, vel qujxima, yujã qujxixima, qujtzontecontia, qujxtelolotia, qujxaiacatia, qujtlactia, qujmatia, qujcxitia: auh yn jquac oiecauh, njmã tepantli itech qujcaltia, vncan qujquetza: auh ynjc amo vetziz, caltech qujquãmjna, aço ica tlaxichtli, anoço ica tepuztlaxichtli.

A. When he hath properly set up his god, then before him he layeth an offering; before him he cutteth his ears, he bleedeth himself, he offereth him prayers. He maketh vows to him. He weepeth before him; he doth penances; he asketh that which is required by him.

A. Jn iquac vel oqujquetz iteouh: njmã ixpan tlamana, ixpan monacaztequj, mjço, qujtlatlauhtia: ivic monetoltia, ixpan choca, tlamaceoa qujtlanjlia, yn jtech monequj.

B. This wretched idolater hath no shame as he calleth [to the god], as he offereth prayers to him who seeth not, who liveth not, who hath no soul. And in order that the sick may recover, he offereth prayers to him; and for the dead, he prayeth to him for life; and for the destitute, he prayeth to him for help; and for the halt, he prayeth to him that they may walk. And he asketh what is required of one who hath nothing, who can offer nothing. It is only wood.

B. Jnjn tlateutocanipul, amo pinaoa in qujnotza, in qujtlatlauhtia, yn amo tlacaquj, in amo tlachia, yn amo iuli, yn atle yanjma: auh yn ipampa inic patiz, qujtlatlauhtia in cucuxquj: auh in jpãpa nemjliztli, qujtlatlauhtia in micquj: yoan qujtlatlauhtia yn atle ynecoca, ynjc qujpaleuiz: auh qujtlatlauhtia, ynjc vel nenemiz, qujtlatlauhtia yn auelnenemj: auh in ie muchi, yn jtech monequj, qujtlanjlia, in atle quipia, yn atle vel qujtemaca içan quaujtl.

Fourteenth Chapter

The wood is good; it is required; it is God's creation. Many things are made of it: of it are made the houses in which we live, and of it are made the boats with which there is the gaining of a livelihood. For these reasons the wood of which is made what we require, what we gain our livelihoods with, is greatly to be valued.

A. But the wood used for idolatry is worthy of being accursed. And he who [so] maketh it, carveth it, is indeed unhappy, indeed to be accursed, even as the wood itself. And the wood-carver must needs be exceedingly accursed because he made that which was not required, which was a great confusion to men. And the wood, greatly required, shall also be accursed, because it is only wood and is worshipped as an idol.

B. And God, our Lord, greatly abhorreth both the idolater and idolatry: him who began idolatry and him who liveth in idolatry. Both will forever be in torment in the land of the dead.

C. These, the demons, were the cause of idolatry. For never will God have mercy upon them. And although they are God's creatures, they must needs be abhorred, accursed, for they are deceivers, tricksters, confusers of men.

D. Those who first introduced idolatry [and] idols dishonored and offended God; thereby they angered God, for thus were very many confused. When the world began, none lived as idolaters; and before the world shall end, idolatry will perish.

E. The witless, the senseless began idolatry here upon earth. But because of their wickedness they suddenly died.

F. Behold how the wicked, the men of little understanding, began idolatry. There lived the son of a man who was ruler, his only son, his youth, whom he loved much. And the youth died. And his father was much saddened thereby; he wept much, he grieved much. And then he commanded that a representation of his beloved son be made, carved of wood or stone. He rigorously commanded the wood-carver to make a true image of him, so that it would be like the painted image of his son. When the repre-

Capitulo quarto decimo.

Jn quaujtl ca qualli, ca monequj, ca itlachioaltzin in dios: ca mjec tlamantli ic muchioa: ca ic muchioa in calli in uncan tinemj, yoan ic muchioa in acalli, ynjc netlaiecultilo: ipampa hi, vellaçotlalonj in quaujtl ynjc muchioa, in totech monequj ynjc titotlaiecultia.

A. Auh in quaujtl ynjc muchioa, in tlateutoqujliztli, vel telchioalonj: auh in qujchioa in qujxima, vel oitlaueliltic, vel telchioalonj, yn jvan in quaujtl: auh in quauhxinquj, monequj cenca telchioaloz, iehica ca oqujchiuh, in amo monequj in cenca tetlapololti: auh in quaujtl, cenca monequj, no telchioaloz: iehica ca çan quaujtl, auh teutoco.

B. Auh in totecujo dios, vntlamanjsti cenca qujmotlaelittilia, yn tlateutocanj, yoan in tlateutoqujliztli: in qujpeoalti tlateutoqujliztli, yoan in tlateutocatinemj, ym umexti mjctlan, cemjcac tlaihijoujltilozque.

C. Jn iehoantin in diablome, oqujpeoaltique in tlateutoqujliztli, ipampa aic qujnmotlaoculiliz in dios: auh maciuj yn jtlachioalhoan dios, monequj cuculilozque, telchioalozque, ca teiztlacaujanjme, teixcuepanjme, tetlapololtianjme.

D. Jn iehoantin vel achto oqujtzintique, in tlateutoqujliztli, in ydolosme, ixtzinco icpactzinco, oeoaque, onenque in dios: ic cēca omoqualanalti in dios, ca cenca mjequjntin ic omotlapololtique: yn jquac otzintic cemanaoac, aiac tlateutocatinenca: auh in aiamo tlamiz cemanaoac, puliuiz in tlateutoqujliztli.

E. Jn tlateutoqujliztli, in aqujmamatcaoaque, in xulopime, oqujtzintique, in nican tlalticpac: auh ipampa yn jntlauelilocaio, iciuhca omjcque.

F. Jzcatquj in quenjn oqujpeoaltique in tlaueliloque, yn aqujmatinj, yn tlateutoqujliztli. Ce tlacatl tlatoanj vnnenca ipiltzin, çan vel izel ipiltzin, itelpuch, in cēca qujtlaçotlaia: auh in telpuchtli, mjc: auh yn jtatzin cenca ic omotequjpacho, cenca chocac, cenca otlaocux: auh njmā otlanaoati, ynjc quaujtl, manoço tetl muchioaz moximaz in jxiptla itlaçopiltzin: oqujtlaquauhnaoati in quauhxinquj, ynjc vel ipatillo qujchioazque, in vel iuhquj iez, yn ipiltzin in tlaixiptlaiotl. Jn oiecauh y, in teixiptla, njman

sentation was done, then he set it up in a good place; there he worshipped it. Then he commanded the people of his household to worship it, and to lay offerings before it — to offer it paper, *copal* [incense], flowers.

G. And in years following the ruler commanded all his vassals to worship the representation of his son and to lay offerings before it. Thus it was that idolatry began.

A. Behold another manner by which idolatry began. Some made representations of those whom they loved who lived in far places. And because they lived in far places, [because] they could not see their bodies, their representations gave them comfort. And they paid them honor, and either the ruler or a noblewoman laid offerings before them.

B. And the painters very carefully painted the representations. Very marvelously, very well they made the representations. Thus they tempted men; thus there was the worship of idols.

C. The painter, or the woodcarver, or the lapidary, or the goldworker, since he greatly wished to quiet doubts, brought it about that what he made was even better than the flesh from which was molded, from which was taken, the representation. The better he formed the representation, the more he confused men.

D. Very many commoners, luckless men, who saw that the representation was very subtly, very carefully made, worshipped it. They thought it was a god. The representation only confused them because it was subtly, carefully made.

E. In this manner were men on earth confused. For because of love or because of honor paid men, they defamed godliness. The precious name of God, which belongeth only to God, they thus gave as name to the representation in stone, in wood.

F. The confusions of the idolaters were not one but many. The confusions arose, lived in idolatry. These [men] thought they were content, but it was in a great war that they lived.

G. These idolaters slew their sons before their gods. And by night they did many things before their gods which sicken and anger one. All their

qualcan oqujquetz, vncan oqujmoteuti: njman oqujnnaoati yn jchan tlaca, in qujmoteutizque, yoan ixpã tlamanazque, qujmanazque yn amatl in copalli, in suchitl.

G. Auh ie iquezqujxiuhioc, otlanaoati in tlatoanj, ynjc ixqujchtin, imaceoalhoan qujmoteutizque, yn ixiptla, yn ipiltzin, yoan ixpan tlamanazque: yujn j, yn otzintic, in tlateutoqujliztli.

A. Izcatquj in oc centlamantli, ynjc otzintic tlateutoqujliztli: cequintin, oqujchiuhque, imixiptlahoan, yn jntlaçohuan in veca nemj: auh in jpampa ca veca nemj, auel qujttaia yn ynnacaio, ytech moiollaliaia yn jmjxiptlaoan: yoan qujnmauiztiliaia, yoan ispan tlamanaia, aço tlatoanj, anoço civapilli.

B. Auh in iehoanti, in tlacujloque, cẽca qujnematcaicujloque in teixiptla, vel mauiztic, vel iectli oqujchiuhque, yn teixiptla, ic oteioleuhque, ynjc oneteutiloc.

C. Jn iehoatl in tlacujlo, yn anoço quauhxinquj, anoço texinquj, anoço teucujtlapitzquj: injc cenca qujiolpachiujtiznequi, yn oqujteq'ti, oc cenca qualli oqujchiuh, yn amo mach iuhquj catca yn jnacaio, yn jtech omocopin, yn jtech omocujc in teixiptla: oc cenca qualli oqujtlali in teixiptla, cenca ic otetlapololtique.

D. Cenca miequjntin, maceoaltin, icnotlaca, yn oqujttaque in teixiptla, in vel mjmati, in vellanematcachioalli, oqujmoteutique: omomatque, ca teutl, çan oqujntlapololti in teixiptla injc mjmati, ynjc tlanematcachioalli.

E. Jhujn yn omotlapololtique, in tlalticpac tlaca: ca ipampa in tetlaçotlaliztli, anoço ipampa in temaviztililiztli, ocaujlqujstique in teuiotl: in tlaçotli tocaitl in teutl, in çan vel izeltzin yaxcatzin in dios, ynjc oqujntocaiotique in teixiptla in tetl, in quaujtl.

F. Jn tlateutocanjme, amo çan centlamantli, in jnnetlapololtiliz ca cenca mjec tlamantli, netlapololtiliztli itech qujça, itech iuli in tlateutoqujliztli: in iehoantin momati ca pacticate, iece vei iauiutl, ipan nemj.

G. Jn iehoantin in tlateutocanjme, qujnmjctia, in jnpilhoan, imjxpan yn inteuhoan: auh cenca mjec tlamantli, in tetlaelti, in tequalanj, in ioaltica quj-

acts, their lives, all were vicious, filthy. They hated one another; they slew one another, they committed adultery one with another. Murder, robbery, adultery, trickery, public disorders, contentions spread everywhere. None saw to gratitude, to chastity. Incontinence, vice, filth were verily the idolaters' way of life.

chioa, yn jmjxpan inteuhoa: in ixqujch in jntlachioal, yn jnnemiliz, muchi teuhio, tlaçollo: nepanotl mocuculia, nepanotl momjctia, nepanutl motlaxima: in temjctiliztli, yn ichtequjliztli, in tetlaximaliztli, in teca necacaiaoaliztli, in necomonjlztli, neisnamiqujliztli, noviian actimotecac: auh aiac qujmocujtlauja in necnelilmatiliztli, in nepializtli, in chipaoacanemjliztli: in haujlnemjliztli, in teuhtli, in tlaçolli, vel innemjliz, in tlateutocanjme.

A. Idolatry is much to be loathed. Its beginning, its start, and its end are in everything evil, improper. And all which is loathsome and confusion, all liveth in, issueth from idolatry.

A. Jn cenca tetlaelti, tlateutoqujliztli, itzin ipeuhca, yoan itzonquizca, yn jxqujch, amo qualli, amo iectli: yoan in jxqujch tetlaelti, yoan in tetlapololti, muchi itech iuli qujça in tlateutoqujliztli.

B. The idolaters, when they take their pleasure, are as if drunk; they become maddened; they talk as if drunk.

B. Jn tlateutocanjme, yn jquac papaquj, iuhqujnma tlaoanque, iollotlaueliloque muchioa, iuhqujn tlaoanque tlatoa.

C. The idolaters, when they put faith in the favor of their gods, do not esteem them. They speak ill of them; they have no fear of them; for they have no souls.

C. Jn tlateutocanjme, in iquac intech tlaquauhtlamati, yn jnteuhoan, çan no atle inpan qujmitta, qujnchicujtoa, amo qujmjmacaci, iehica ca atle yn inanjma.

D. Many such things come to pass among the idolaters. Not without cause doth God, the only God, abominate them. But they greatly honor their false gods. And they are much given to false oaths in order to deceive one. But they esteem no true justice.

D. Jn izqujtlamantli in, inpan muchioa tlateutocanjme: amo çan nen ca oqujnmotelchiujli in dios icel teutl: auh yn imiztlacateuhoan, cenca qujmauiztilique. Auh in iztlaca juramento, cenca itech omomatque, injc teca omocacaiauhque: auh in melaoac iusticia atle ipan qujttaque.

E. Oaths should not be habitual. Those who often call upon His holy name commit a sin. It is not required that His holy name be called upon twice, for the reason that it is great; it is greatly required. He who falsely calleth upon His holy name committeth a sin. It shall be his last sin.

E. Jn iuramento, amo monequi itech nemachoz: in aqujque miecpa qujteneoa itocatzin, tlatlacoa: ca amo monequi vpa moteneoaz, yn iteutocatzin, in jpan vei, yn ipan in cenca monequj: in çan tlapicq' teneoa yn jtocatzin tlatlacua, qujtzacutiaz in itlatlacul.

Chapter Twelve

Alas, O our Lord God, thy heart is completely good, completely tender. All that Thou bringest about for all of us, who are the people of the world, all is good, all is righteous. And because Thy heart is very good, Thou dost not at once destroy sinners, Thou dost not at once consume them with fire: Thou only instructest them yet, Thou warnest them to leave their evil life, to be satisfied in Thee.

Capitulo. 12.

Jioiave, totecujoe diose, in moiollotzin, ca cenquizca qualli, cenqujzca iamanquj: in jxqujch in topan ticmuchiujlia in timuchinti, in cemanaoac titlaca, ca muchi qualli, muchi melaoac: auh ipampa ca cenca qualli moiollotzin, in tlatlacoanj, amo njman tiqujnmopopolhuja amo njman tiqujnmotlatlatilia, çan oc tiqujnmonemachtilia, tiqujmononochilia, ynjc qujcaoazque, yn jmaqualnemiliz, ynjc motetzinco pachiuizque.

A. O our Lord, these idolaters who lived on Thy earth Thou hast much abominated because of their evil life, because what they were wont to do aroused

A. Totecujoe, in iehoantin tlateutocanjme, in motlalpantzinco nemja, cenca otiqujnmotlaelittili, yn ipampa yn imaqualnemiliz: ipampa ca cenca tequa-

men's anger, offended them. For they were wont to be soothsayers, to steal other's goods, to practise divination by means of knotted cords, to practise divination by strewing grains of dried maize. And they slew things before the devils, the demons, and they slew their sons; with them the debt was paid before carved stone, carved wood. And they ate the flesh of men. Thou hast waited long for these to turn from their evil lives. But because they wished not to turn from their lives, Thou hast destroyed them. Thy vassals the Christians brought to an end their wickedness; they conquered them.

B. O our Lord, since Thou hast so done this, will one say something? Will one say, "Why hast Thou so done this?" And will one dispute with Thee because Thou hast so done this? Will one avenge himself on Thee because of the punishment of the evil, the unrighteous? And if Thou shalt destroy all the idolaters on earth, will one speak? Will one say, "Why didst Thou thus?" For all of them are thy creatures.

C. There is no other God, there is no other Creator. For Thou only art God; for Thou alone commandest all things which are in heaven, which are on earth. And when Thou givest judgment, it is righteous. No great ruler, no great emperor shall question Thee, shall say to Thee, "Why hast Thou slain, hast Thou consumed my vassals?"

D. O our Lord, Thou art wholly good, everything that Thou dost is all righteous, all good, for this reason: because Thou art almighty, all is fulfilled in Thee, all which is good, righteous. And because Thy holy name reacheth everywhere, Thou hast mercy everywhere.

E. O our Lord, Thou makest known Thy might, Thy power to the idolaters who wish not to believe in Thy eternal might, Thy eternal power. Hence Thou increasest their misery even more, because of their disobedience. O Lord, Thine is perfect, great might, and Thou hast the might at once to destroy sinners when they offend Thee. And Thou dost in no way so do this, but still waitest that in peace they may change their lives.

Chapter Fifteen

Thou, Who art God, Who art our God, Who art our Ruler: very tender, very good is Thy heart. And

lanj, teiolitlaco, in qujchiuhtinenca: ca tonalpouhtinenca, tetlacujcujlitinēca, mecatlapouhtinenca, tlaulchaiauhtinenca. Auh in tlatlacateculo in tzitzitzimi imjxpan tlamictiaia: yoã yn jnpilhoan qujnmictiaia, inca mostlaoaia, yn imjspan, in tetlaxinti, in quauhtlaxinti: yoan qujquaia in tlacanacatl: in iehoantin jn vecauhtica tiqujnmuchieli: ynjc qujcuepazque yn jmaqualnemjliz: auh ipampa yn amo qujnecque in qujcuepazque yn jnnemiliz otiqujnmopupulhuj, oqujtzacutiaque, yn jntlauelilocaio, oqujnpopoloque in momaceoaltzitzinhoan in x̃pianome.

B. Totecujoe ynic oiuhticmuchiujli, yn, cuix aca itla qujtoz? Cuix aca qujtoz, tleica yn iuh ticmuchiujlia, in? auh cuix aca mitzmotlatzoviliz? in ipampa iuh ticmuchiujli? auh cujx aca motetzinco motzoncuiz, yn ipampa intlatzacujltiloca, yn aqualti, yn aiecti? auh intla tiqujnmopopolhuiz, yn jxq'chtin cemanaoac tlateutocanjme, cujs aca tlatoz? cujx aca qujtoz, tleica in iuh ticmuchiujlia? ca muchinti motlachioaltzitzinhoan.

C. Niman aiac vnca, oc ce teutl, nimã aiac oc ce tlachioale, ca çan moceltzin titeutl, ca çan moceltzin ticmopachilhuja, yn jsqujch yn jlhujcac onoc, in tlalticpac, onoc: auh ynjc timotetlatzontequjlilia, ca vel melaoac, njman aiac vei tlatoanj, in anoço vei Emperador, mitzmotlatlanjliz, mitzmolhuiliz: tleicâ otiqujnmomjctili, otiqujnmotlatlatili, in nomaceoalhoan?

D. Totecujoe, iehica ca ticenquizca qualli, yn jsquich ticmuchiujlia, muchi melaoac, muchi qualli: ipampa ca muchi moueli, motetzinco cenquiztoc, yn isqujch qualli, melaoac: auh ipampa ca novijan aci, in motlatocaiotzin, novjian timotetlaoculilia.

E. Totecujoe, in mouelitilitzin, in muchicaoaliztzin, ticmonestilia, in impan tlateutocanjme: in amo qujneltocaznequj, in cemanqui movelitilitzin, yn cemanqui, muchicaoaliztzin: ynjc oc cenca tiqujnmoveililia yn jnnetoliniliz, yn ipampa intzõtetiliz: Totecujoe ca maxcatzin, in cenquizquj in vei in velitiliztli: auh ca timovelitilia, yn njman tiqujnmopolhuiz, in tlatlacoanj, yn jquac mitzmoiolitlacalhuja: auh ynjn ca amo iuh ticmuchiujlia, ca çan oc tiqujnmuchielia, ynjc iviian qujcuepazque yn jnnemjliz.

Capitulo. 15.

Jn tehoatzin, in tidios, in titoteuh, in titotlatocatzin, cenca iamanquj, cenca qualli moiollotzin: auh

everything which Thou dost is all good, all righteous. And in Thy mercy Thou hast set in order all creatable things.

A. O our Lord, we understand that we are Thine, we Christians. If we shall sin, we still belong to Thee. We know Thou art perfectly great, perfectly good. And if we shall not sin, we know we are with Thee, for we are Thy chosen ones.

B. O our Lord, the knowledge of Thee hath been well revealed; it hath saved men. And by the keeping of Thy commandments is eternal life merited.

Chapter Sixteen

O our Lord God, the lives and the deaths of our bodies are of Thy making, of Thy knowledge. The life of peace and the life of misery of our bodies are in Thy hand.

A. But the death of our souls is not of Thy creation, not of Thy establishing. For only we, we people, by our sins, by our wickedness kill our souls, cast them into the land of the dead. And when our soul abandoneth our body, it is not possible that it again enter within it. All will be therewith ended forever, for it went forth for the last time; it went for the last time either to the good place or else not to the good place. There they will be together, where we have our places. And no one who is in Thy hand will resist, for Thou art almighty, for Thou art everywhere.

B. The idolaters who will not acknowledge Thee, by the might of Thy hand Thou punishest; with water, with hailstones, with fire Thou hast destroyed them.

[Confutation of Idolatry][166]

The aforementioned word of God which hath been spread before you, my beloved children, hath given very strong light to men; it hath made them see. Thus it will be known that idolatry bringeth confusion to men; it will cast them into the land of the dead; it is a great sin against God, our Creator, our Redeemer.

And now, that their doubts may indeed be satisfied, since they are of weak character, it is still re-

in jxqujch in ticmuchiujlia, muchi qualli, muchi melaoac: auh ca motetlaoculiliztica, ticmotecpanjlia, yn ixqujch chioalonj.

A. Totecujoe, ca iuh qujmattica in toiollo, ca timaxcatzitzinhoan, in tixp̃ianome: intla titlatlacozque, ca ça oc motetzinco tipouj: ticmati ca ticenquizca vei, ticenquizca qualli: auh intlacamo titlatlacozque, ticmati ca motlantzinco ticate: ca timotlapepenaltzitzinhoan.

B. Totecujoe, yn miximachocatzin, ca vel tetlanestili, vel temaqujsti: auh yn ipialoca, yn motenaoatiltzin, ic icnopilhujlo, in cemjcac nemjliztli.

Capitulo. 16.

Totecujoe diose, ca tehoatzin, vel moneiocultzin, momachitzin, yn jiuliliz, yoã imiquiz in tonacaio: yn jpaccanemjliz yoan yn jcuculiz in tonacaio, ca momactzinco ca.

A. Auh yn imjquiz, in tanjma, amo motlachioaltzin, amo motlatlaliltzin: ca çan tehoanti, in titlaca, totlatlacultica, totlavelilocaiotica, ticmjctia in tanjma, mjctlan tictlaça. Auh yn iquac, yn tanjma qujtlalcahuja in tonacaio, auelitiz in oc cepa itic calaquiz, yn jxqujchica tlamiz cemanaoac, ca oiccenquiz, oiccenia: in anoço qualcan, yn acanoço qualcan, vmpa ceniez yn vmpa oticmoieiantili: auh ca njman aiac momacpatzinco momapatlaz: iehica ca muchi moueli, ca noviian timoietzinotica.

B. Jn tlateutocanjme, yn amo mitzmomachitocaznequj, mocenmacca velitiliztica, tiqujnmotlatzacujltilia, atica, teciuhtica, yoan tletica, otiqujnmopopulhuj.

Jn teutlatolli omoteneuh, in amispan omomelauh, notlaçopilhoane: ca cenca chicaoac vel tetlanextili, tetlachialti. Jnjc vel iximachoz, in tlateutoquiliztli, in ca cenca tetlapololti: vel mictlan tetlaz, vel vei yoilitlaculocatzin in dios, in toteiocuxcatzin, totemaquisticatzin.

Auh yn axcan ynjc vel iniollo pachiuiz, yn amo cenca chicaoac in imjx, yn iniollo, oc monequj oc

166. Sahagún's "Confutations" begin without heading in the *Florentine Codex*.

quired that I spread out the word of God, written above, so that all men shall know it. For idolatry is much to be abominated, despised.

achi njcmelaoaz, in teutlatolli, in tlacpac omjcuilo ynjc muchi tlacatl qujmatiz, ca in tlateutoqujliztli, cenca vellaelittalonj, telchioalonj.

A. Perceive, my children, the light, the torch by which will be known the only God, God through Whom we live; for this is the word of God. And knowledge of the false gods whom the ancients worshipped likewise issueth from the declaration of God's word. This word of God lieth folded in the bosom, in the womb of the Holy Church, our mother, like the gold of heaven, the emeralds of heaven, the turquoise, the gems, the precious stones which belong to her, which exceed all things in preciousness, in being worthy of guarding. This word of God, which all desire in order to be saved, is greatly required by all who willingly believe in it, because the word of God is a light; it is a torch. God the Father, the Son, the Holy Ghost hath given, hath guarded our mother, the Holy Church, that she may give light to, may teach all her children.

A. Tla xicmocaqujtican, notlaçopilhoane, yn tlanextli, yn ocutl, ynjc vel iximachoz, yn izel teutl ipalnemoanj dios: ca iehoatl in teutlatolli. Auh yn jmiximachoca yn iztlacateteu, in qujnmoteutiaque, in vevetque: çan no itech quiça yn jmelaoaca, in teutlatolli. Jnjn teutlatlatolli ixillantzinco, itozcatlantzinco, in tonantzin sancta yglesia, cuecuelpachiuhtoc, iuhqujnma ilhujcac teucujtlatl, ilhujcac quetzalitztli, teuxiujtl, temaquiztli, tlaçotetl ipam pouj: in vellapanauja ynjc tlaçotli, ynjc pialonj: ynjn teutlatolli, yn jsqujchtin momaqujxtiznequj, cenca intech monequj, in iollocopa qujneltocazque: iehica ca dios itlatoltzin, ca tlanestli, ca ocotl. Jn dios tetatzin, in tepiltzin, in espiritu sancto, qujmomaqujli, qujmopialtili, yn tonantzin sancta yglesia, ynjc qujntlanextilia, qujnmachtia, yn jsqujchtin ipilhoan.

B. My children, perceive that God's word is God's light. By it those who live in darkness will be able to see — those who have lost the way, idolaters who live following the lying words of the devil, who is indeed the father of lies. And that their gods, their rulers be made known to them, the word of God, the word of truth, hath been declared to them. Because above I have told, above I have said the word of God, in which it is revealed, it is declared, how idolatry began. Likewise here are revealed many of the confusions, miseries, blindnesses into which the idolaters fell.

B. Tla xicmocaqujtican, notlaçopilhoane, in teutlatolli, ca teutlanestli: ynjc vellachiazque in tlaiooaian nemj, in mixcueptinemj, yn tlateutocanjme, qujtocatinemj ymiztlacatlatol in diablo, yn vel yta in iztlacatiliztli. Auh ynjc vel qujmiximachilizque, yn jnteouh, yn jntlatocauh, in qujmotenqujstili in teutlatolli, yn neltiliztlatolli: ipampa in tlacpac, onjcteneuh, in tlacpac onjqujto, in teutlatolli, yn vncan neztica, melaoatica, yn quenjn otzintic opeuh, in tlateutoqujliztli; no yoan vncan neztica, in ca mjec tlamantli, netlapololtiliztli, netoliniliztli, ixpopuiutiliztli, ipan ovetzque yn tlateutocanjme.

C. This word of God, the light of God, instructeth us, notifieth us that it is in no way possible that there be many gods. There is only one, the only Creator by Whom we live, ruler everywhere. And in the word of God, which hath been written above, is revealed, behold: *Non est enim alius deus quam tu, cui cura est de omnibus.* That is to say, "O our Lord God, Thou alone art God, thou art ruler. None else is God, none else is ruler. In Thy hand alone are all things visible [and] invisible."

C. Jn iehoatl in teutlatolli, in teutlanextli, techmachtia techcaqujtia, ca njman amo velitiz, in mjequjntin iezque teteu, ca çan vel çe, in çan vel izeltzin, teiocuianj, ipalnemoanj, novian, tlatoanj: auh in teutlatolli yn tlacpac omjcujlo, itech neztica, izcatquj. Non est enjm alius deus quam tu, cuj cura est de omnibus. q. n. Totecujoe, diose, ca çan mozeltzin titeutl, titlatoanj, aiac oc ce teutl, aiac oc ce tlatoanj: çan mozeltzin momactzinco ca, yn jxqujch ittalo, yn amo yttalo.

D. This is thus revealed: Huitzilopochtli is no god; Tezcatlipoca is no god; Tlaloc, or Tlalocatecutli, is no god; Quetzalcoatl is no god, neither is Ciuacoatl a goddess; Chicomecoatl is no goddess, neither is Teteo innan a goddess; Tzapotlan tenan is no

D. Jnin ca ic vel neztica, ca amo teutl, in vitzilubuchtli: amo teutl, in tezcatlipuca, amo teutl in tlaloc, yn anoço tlalocatecutli: amo teutl in quetzalcoatl: amono teutl, in cioacoatl: amo teutl in chicome coatl; amono teutl, yn teteu innan: amo teutl, in tza-

goddess, nor are the Ciuapipilti or Ciuateteo goddesses, nor is Chalchiuhtli icue a goddess, nor is Uixtociuatl a goddess, nor is Tlaçolteotl a goddess. Xiuhtecutli is no god, Macuilxochitl is no god, nor is Omacatl a god, nor is Ixtlilton Tlaltetecuin a god, nor is Opochtli a god, nor is Xipe totec a god. Yiacatecutli is no god; Chiconquiauitl is no god; Chalmeca ciuatl is no goddess; Acxomocuil is no god; Nacxitl is no god; Cochimetl is no god; Yacapitzauac is no god; Napa tecutli is no god; the Tepictoton are not gods; the sun is no god; the moon, the stars — none is a god; Tlaltecutli is no god; the water of the sea, the ocean, is no god. But all, here in New Spain, were worshipped in times past. None of them is a god. For all are demons, evil spirits, as it is in the word of God: *Omnes dii gentium demonia*; that is to say, All whom the idolaters worship, all are devils, demons, evil spirits.

E. Unhappy are they who worshipped these demons, for they are full of evil; they are wicked; they are the adversaries, the affliction of us, the people of the earth. Unhappy are they who offered up to them the blood of their children, the hearts of their fellows. Unhappy are those who prayed humbly to them, who kissed the earth in the presence of the devils and their representations in order to ask what they required. They fooled themselves greatly when they thought that these really gave them all wealth, all riches; and that these aided, defended, and saved men. Those who thought this, your forefathers, much confused themselves and much confused others. And because they would thus attain what their hearts required, they laid offerings before the devils; they fasted, they passed all-night vigils, they bled themselves, they prayed. In many ways they thus afflicted, they thus tormented their bodies in the presence of the devils, the demons. Moreover, they offered them many gifts; their gifts took the form of green stones, quetzal feathers — spreading, curving, truly green; and costly mantles, costly vestments. And before them they laid offerings of various flowers and many kinds of incense. Such they did in order to pay honor to their adversaries, their enemies, those who ill-treated them — who required no honor, who required no love. For they required only to be abominated, abhorred, hated. Therefore are eternally condemned, eternally accursed the adversaries of our Lord God and the adversaries of us the people.

putla tena: amono teteu, in cioapipilti, anoço cioateteu: amono teutl in chalchiuhtli, icue; amono teutl, in vixtocioatl: amono teutl in tlaçulteutl: amo teutl in xiuhtecutli: macuilsuchitl amo teutl; vmacatl amono teutl: istlilton, tlaltetecujn, amono teutl: in opuchtli, amono teutl: xipe totec amono teutl: yiacatecutli amo teutl: chicũquiavitl amo teutl: chalmeca cioatl amo teutl: in acxumocujl amo teutl: nacxitl amo teutl: cochimetl amo teutl: in iacapitzaoac amo teutl: in napa tecutli amo teutl: tepictoton, amo teteu: yn tonatiuh amo teutl: in metztli, in cicitlaltin aiac teutl: in tlaltecutli amo teutl, yn teuatl, yn ilhujcaatl, amo teutl. Auh yn ie muchintin, yn nican nueua españa, neteutiloia, ie vecauh, njman aiac teutl: ca muchintin tzitzitzimj, culeleti: iuh ca in teutlatolli. Omnes dij gentium demonja: qujtoznequj. Jn isqujchtin, yn qujnmoteutia, yn tlateutocanjme, muchintin, diablome, tzitzitzimj, culeleti.

E. Ointlaueliltic, in qujnmoteutitiaque in iehoantin in tzitzitzimi, ca uel qujmaxiltique tlaueliloque, vel toiaohoan, vel totecuculicahoan, in tlalticpac titlaca. Ointlaueliltic in qujnmacaque, yn jmezço, yn inpilhoan, yn jniollo, in jnvampoan: yn iehoantin jn ointlaueliltic, in qujmicnotlatlauhtiaia, in jmispan tlalquaia, in diablosme: yoan yn jmixiptlaoan ynic qujmjtlaniliaia, in tlein intech monequja: cenca moztlacaujaia, ynic momatia ca in iehoantin, vel qujtemaca, in jsqujch in tetlamachti, in isqujch tecujltono. Yoan ca no iehoanti, tepaleuja, temanauja, yoan temaqujstia: in iuh momatque hi, in amoculhoan, cenca omotlapololtique, yoan cenca otetlapololtique. Auh yn ipampa injc vel qujcnopilhuizque, in tlein qujnequja iniollo: imispan tlamanaia in diablome, moçaoaia, istoçoaia, mĵçoia tlatlatlauhtiaia, mjec tlamantli ynjc qujtoneoaia, ynjc qujchichinatzaia in jnnacaio, in jmispan in diablome, in tzitzitzimj: no yoan cenca mjec tlamantli ventli, in qujmanaia: invẽ muchioaia in chalchiujtl, in quetzalli, in patlaoac, in vitoliuhquj, in vel xopaleoac: yoan in tlaçotilmatli, in tlaçotlãquj. Yoan imjxpan qujmanaia, in nepapan xuchitl: yoan miec tlamantli, in copalli: in juh qujchioaia hi, ca ic qujnmauiztiliaia in jniaohoan, yn jntecuculicaoan, yn jntetolinjcaoa: in atle intech monequj mavizçotl, yn atle intech momonequj tetlaçotlaliztli: ca çan monequj cenca telchioalozque, tlaellitalozque, cuculilozque: iehica ca tlacemjsnanaoatilti, tlacentelchioalti: yiaohoan yn totecujo dios, yoan toiaohoan in titlaca.

F. Unhappy and much to be blamed are those who even now live as idolaters, yet whom God's word hath come to reach, yet by whom the Holy Gospel is heard. Even more are to be wept, to be severely reprimanded, those who have already been baptized, who during the time of their baptism once again practise soothsaying, cast auguries in water, believe in dreams, or else their voices sing, their eyelids flutter, or else they hold the barn owl, the owl as an omen. And even more in times past was there terror over omens. All who do so must here on earth meet torment, and when they shall die, they shall be cast into the land of the dead.

G. Because of idolatry, much misery befell the old people — your grandfathers, your grandmothers. There were many wars in New Spain when there still was idolatry; frequent famine, frequent pestilence were widespread; thus there was dying. And therefore did the Spaniards come to conquer, therefore many of the common folk perished; for all came to pass because of idolatry. And now misery prevaileth, all because of idolatry, for it is not yet completely forgotten. Our Lord God is exceeding wroth; He consumeth the idolaters with fire. For idolatry offendeth our Lord God; it is the worst of all sins. And as for the idolaters there in the land of the dead, even more terrible is their place of torment — their weeping, their tears, their cries, which shall never cease. It is written in God's word.

A. Behold the cries, the tears of the idolaters: *Erravimus in via veritatis*, etc. (*Wisdom*, Chapter 5). That is to say, "Unhappy we, for we erred while we were living on earth, and the straight road of righteous life we saw not; the sun of righteous life did not give us light; our sinful way tired us, it exhausted us;[167] and our road to ruin vexed us; our sins put us into dangerous places. Of what advantage to us were pride, greatness? Of what advantage to us was riches on earth? All such things, like smoke, [like] shadows, fall in confusion; they are like the messenger running fast; like the boat rapidly gliding as if driven by the wind of which nothing is seen whence it issued; like the bird which hasteneth greatly as it flieth, which goeth leaving no trace;

F. Ocelintlaueliltic, ca cenca tlacemjsnaoatilti, in iehoantin in oc noma tlateutocatinemj in axcan, in ie oacico teutlatolli, in ie caco in sancto Evãgelio: ca oc cenca techoctique, tetozqujtenque, in iehoantin in ie omoquatequjque, yn ipan in jnnequatequjliz, in ie no ceppa tlapoa, atlan teitta, qujneltoca in temjctli, anoço intozquj choca, ymjs papatlaca: anoço qujmotetzavia in chiquatli, in teculotl: yoan oc cequj in ie vecauh netetzaujloia. Jn jsq'chtin, yn iuhquj qujchioa yn, cenca monequj in njcan tlalticpac, tlaihiioujltilozque, yoan yn jquac miquizque, mjctlan tlaçalozque.

G. Jn ipampa tlateutoqujliztli, cenca mjec tlamantli netoliniliztli, impã muchioaia in veuetque, yn amoculhoan, yn amocihoan: ca mjec tlamantli iauiotl, njcan manca, in nueua españa, yn oc ipan tlateutoqujliztli: miecpa, maianaloia, miecpa cuculiztli momanaia, ic mjcooaia. Auh inic tepeoaco inin españoles, jnjc miequjnti ispoliuhque in maceoalti, ca muchi ipampa omuchiuh, in tlateutoqujliztli: auh yn axcan yn izqujtlamantli tetoliniliztli manj, ca muchi ipampa in tlateutoqujliztli, iehica, ca aiamo cemjlcauj: Jn totecujo dios, tlapanauja ynic moqualanaltia, ca qujnmotlatlatilia, in tlateutocanjme: iehica ca in intlateutoqujliz ynjc qujmoiolitlacalvia in totecujo dios, vel quipanauja, yn jsqujch tlatlaculli. Auh in tlateutocanjme, in vmpa mictlan, oc cenca temamauhti, yn jntlaihiioujltiloca: yn jnchoquiz, yn jmjxaio, yn jnchoquiztlatol, yn aic vel qujcaoazque: ca teutlatolpan ycujliuhtoc.

A. Jzcatquj yn inchoquiz, yn imixaio in tlateutocanjme. Erraujmus in via veritatis, etc. Sapientie, 5 capitulo. qujtoznequj. Ototlaueliltic ca otitiscuepque, yn oc tlalticpac tinenca: auh in melaoac iecnemilizvtli, amo tiqujttaque, in iecnemiliztonatiuh, amo techtlanextili, otechtlaciavilti, otecianmjcti, in totlatlaculvuj: auh yn tonetlapololtilizvuj cenca otechama, cenca ovican otechaquj, in totlatlacul: tle otechonqujsti, in nepoaliztli, in tlatocaiutl? tle otechonqujsti, in tlalticpac necujltonoliztli? Jn izqujtlamantli hi, iuhqujma puctli ceoalli, ompoliuhtiuetzi: iuhqujnma titlantli in cenca totocatiqujça: iuhqujnma acalli, in cenca totocatiuh, in juhquj êcatoco, yn amo tle neci in campa quiça: iuhqujnma tototl, in cẽca totoca injc patlanj, yn atle icximachio qujcauh-

167. Probably *otecianmicti* is to be read *otechcianmicti.*

like the bird-arrow which right swiftly reacheth its mark, nor is it seen whence it issued. Thus it befell us on earth, for we were living but a moment on earth, we swiftly brought our lives to a close because of our sins; our lives ended, perished."

tiuh: iuhqujnma totomjtl, in vel iciuhca onacitiuetzi, amono neci, in campa oquiz: O ca iuhquj otopanomuchiuh, in tlalticpac, ca çan achintoca tlalticpac otonnēque, çan iciuhca ontzonquiz, in tonemjliz, yn ipampa in totlatlacul, ovntlan, vmpoliuh in tonemjliz.

B. Like these are the words of the idolaters, like these their weeping, their tears, their words of grief, their words of lamentation, which shall never be comforted. But those who know, who obey our Lord God shall attain His Kingdom, His riches, because our Lord God is perfectly enriching. Thus is the word of God, as hath been told above.

B. O ca iuhquj hi, yn intlatol in tlateutocanjme, iuhqui in, yn inchoquiz, yn jmixaio, yn intlaocullatol, yn jnchoquiztlatol, yn njman aic vel moiollalizque. Auh in qujmiximachilia, in qujmotlacamachitia, yn totecujo dios, qujcnopilhuizque, yn jtlatocaiotzin, yn jnecujltonoliztzin: iehica ca cenquizca mocujltonoanj, yn totecujo dios, iuh ca in teutlatolli in tlacpac omjto.

C. Behold, once more I declare unto you: *O quam bonus et quam suavis est domine spiritus tuus in omnibus*, etc. That is, "Alas, O our Lord God, Thou art perfectly good and Thou art tender of heart. Thou greatly lovest all of us."

Thus it can be declared, that is, "O our Lord God, Thy love is of the Holy Ghost; it is almighty. And Thou sendest over us the goodness, the grace, the softness of Thy love. Thou hast made all that is good, proper, in Thy creatures, so that it will be of advantage to us. And also Thou Thyself art a gift to us people. Thus it is plain, thus we know that Thou art greatly merciful. For Thou offerest us Thy faith, that we may know Thee. And Thou offerest us Thy commandments that we may obey Thee. And Thou offerest us Thy Sacraments, that we may restore, purify, and that we may strengthen our souls. Thus shall we attain eternal life there in Heaven.

C. Izcatquj ie no cepa namechmelavilia O quam bonus et quam suaujs est domjne spiritus tuus in omnibus, etc. qujtoznequj. Yioiaue, totecujoe diose, ca ticenquizca qualli, auh ca cenca iamanquj in moiollotzin, cenca titechmotlaçotilia yn timuchinti.

Jnic vel momelaoa, q'toznequj. Jio totecujoe diose, in motetlaçotlalitzin, ca iehoatzin in espiritu sancto, ca muchi ueli: auh ca topan quivalmjoalia, yn iqualtiliz, yn jiectiliz aviiaca in motetlaçotlalitzin: oticmuchiujlitzino, yn isqujch in qualli, in iectli in intech ca yn motlachioaltzitzinhoan: ynjc muchi techpaleuiz in titlaca: auh ca no vel tehoatzin titonemactzin in titlaca, ynjc neci, ynjc ticmati, ca cenca timotetlaoculilianj: iehica ca titechmomaqujlia yn moneltococatzin, ynjc vel timitztiximachilizque: yoan titechmomaqujlia yn motenaoatiltzin, injc vel timitztouellamachtilizque: yoan titechmomaqujlia in mosacramentotzin, ynjc ticmopatilia, yoã ticmuchipavilia, yoan ynic ticmuchicavilia in tanjma: inic vel tiqujcnopilhuizque, in cemicac nemjliztli, in vmpa ilhujcac:

"And Thou further showest Thy mercy. For Thy servants who offend Thee Thou destroyest not now, Thou castest into the flames not now; Thou admonishest them gently, Thou warnest them gently, that they may change their lives. By Thy words Thy preachers admonish sinners, and Thy priests give them the Sacraments that they may change their lives and that they may satisfy Thee. And those who wish not to know Thee, who wish not to cease idolatry, them Thou castest into the land of the dead. And those who believe in Thee[168] who wish not to

yoan oc cenca ticmonextilia in motetlaoculilitzin: ca in iehoanti yn momaceoaltzitzinoan, in mjtzmoiolitlacalhuja, amo njman tiqujnmopopolhuja, amo njman tiqujnmotlatlatilia, çan iujan tiqujnmononochilia, çan ivian tiqujnmonemachtilia: injc vel qujcuepazque yn jnnemiliz: ca motēcopatzinco, in motemachticaoan, qujnnonotza in tlatlacoanj: auh in moteupiscatzitzinhoan, qujnmaca in sacramentos, ynjc vel qujcuepazque in jnnemiliz, yoã injc vel motetzinco pachiuizque. Auh yn amo mitzmjximachiliznequj, yn amo qujcaoaliztlamati, in tlateutoqujliztli,

168. Corresponding Spanish text reads: *"y a los que no os qujeren conocer."* The negative is missing in the Nahuatl.

change their lives, who die in sin, them Thou punishest with eternal torment there in the land of the dead. And this Thou dost in such wise that it is all righteous. None may change Thy word; none may reverse Thy word. Neither they who dwell in Heaven nor the people on earth, none can say, 'Why dost Thou do this?' Thy word is not to be changed. For what Thou customarily dost is righteous, and Thou art the fount of life, the fount of good, the fount of might. In Thee lie complete riches, all glory, all contentment. And Thou rulest everywhere; and all that is good, proper, issueth from Thee. Thou alone givest them."

D. Thus it is very plain, my dear children, how much worthy of love, [how] much worthy of honor is our Lord God. For he is the One through Whom there is life, our Creator, ruler everywhere.

Likewise it is plain, above, what manner of gods were those of your forefathers — very wicked, deceivers, tricksters, haters of men, worthy of being abhorred, of being scorned.

E. Now it is required that you hear the history of each of those who were your forefathers' gods, that their wickedness may be plain.

The ancients, who were well apprised, related to us, [and] we have newly instructed you, how there was worship of Huitzilopochtli everywhere in the land of Mexico. He was indeed the god of the Mexicans. But this Huitzilopochtli, we know, was a common man, a sorcerer, an omen of evil, a madman, a deceiver, a creator of war, a war-lord. He cast at men the turquoise serpent, the fire drill — war. For this Huitzilopochtli, verily the devil's man, your grandparents celebrated a feast day thrice each year. War captives were slain, ceremonially bathed slaves were offered up; they shed much blood there at Itepeyoc. Many acts of confusion they performed before his image. This, which much confused, much terrified, much shamed men, your grandparents proceeded to do.

F. Likewise we know that in times past, everywhere here in New Spain, there was worship of Tezcatlipoca. And they [also] named him Titlacauan, and Yaotl, Necoc yaotl, Moyocoya, Neçaualpilli. This Tezcatlipoca, the ancients went on to say, was a

mjctlan tiqujnmotlaxiliia: yoan in motlaneltocacaoan in amo qujcuepaznequj, yn innemjliz, in çan ipan miq' yn intlatlacul, cemicac tlaihiioujliztli, ic tiqujnmotlatzacujltilia, in vmpa mictlan: auh ynjn yn iuh ticmuchivilia in, ca muchi melaoac, çan njman, aiac qujcuepaz in motlatoltzin, aiac mitzmotlatolilochtiliz: yn aço ilhujcac chaneque, yn anoço tlalticpactlaca, aiac vel qujtoz, tleica in iuh ticmuchiujlia hi? njman amo cuepalonj, in motlatoltzin: iehica, ca cenca melaoac in ticmuchivilianj, yoan ca tinemjlizameialli, tiqualtilizameialli, tiuelitilizameialli, motetzinco cenqujztoc, yn isqujch tecujltono, yn ixqujch tetlamachti, yn jsqujch tepapaqujlti: auh ca tehoatzin, novian timotlatocatilia: yoan in jsqujch in qualli iectli, motechpatzinco quiça, çan moceltzin ticmotemaqujlia.

D. Jc cenca vel neztica, notlaçopilhoane, in quenjn cenca tlaçotlalonj, cenca mauiztililonj in totecujo dios: iehica ca ipalnemoanj, teiocoianj, noujan tlatoanj:

çan no tlacpac neztica, in quenamique inteuan, yn amocolhoan: cenca vellaveliloque, teiztlacaujanj, teca mocacaiaoanj, tecuculianj, vellaelittalonj, vel telchioalonj.

E. Jn axcan vel monequj, in anqujcaquizque cecẽiaca intlatollo, yn jnteuan catca, yn amoculhoan: ynjc vel neciz in jntlauelilocaio.

Jn iehoantin yn ueuetque, in vel machiceque, otechcaqujtique, in tehoantin, in vel iancujcan otamechmachtique, in quenjn oneteutiloc in Vitzilobuchtli: noviian in tlalpan in mexica, vel inteouh in mexica. Auh ynjn vitzilobuchtli, ticmati, ca maceoalli, naoalli, tetzaujtl, atlacacemelle, teiscuepanj, qujiocuianj, iauiotl, iautecani: tepan qujtlaça in xiuhcoatl, in mamalhuaztli, in iauiotl, in teuatl, in tlachinolli: Jnin Vitzilobuchtli, in vel ymaceoal in diablo, in amoculhoan quilviquixtiliaia, espan cecexiujtl: malmjcoaia, tlaaltilmjcoaia: cenca miec eztli noquiuja, in vncan itepeioc: miec tlamantli netlapololtiliztli quichioaia, ispan in ixiptla. Jnin, cenca tetlapololti, cenca teiçauj, cenca tepinauhti, in oqujchiuhtiaque yn amoculhoan.

F. No yoan ticmati, ca njcan noujan nueua españa ie uecauh, oneteutiloc in tezcatlipuca: yoan qujtocaiotique, titlacaoan, yoan iautl, necoc iautl, moiocoia, neçaoalpilli. Jnjn tezcatlipuca qujtotiaque in veuetque, vel teutl, noujan ynemjan, mictlan, tlalticpac,

true god; his abode was everywhere — in the land of the dead, on earth, in heaven. When he walked upon the earth he quickened war; he quickened vice, filth; he brought anguish, affliction to men; he brought discord among men, wherefore he was called "the enemy on both sides." He mocked men, he ridiculed men. He was called wind, shadow. This wicked Tezcatlipoca, we know, is Lucifer, the great devil who there in the midst of Heaven, even in the beginning, began war, vice, filth. From there he was cast out, from there he fell. But he walketh here upon the earth deceiving men, tricking men. For so is the word of God: *Factum est proelium magnum in coelo.* Apoc., 12. That is, a great war was fought in the midst of Heaven, which Lucifer began. This Tezcatlipoca Titlacauan is a great devil. The ancients worshipped him, and they celebrated his feast day when [it was the month of] Toxcatl, and they slew his representation, whom they named Titlacauan. So much were the ancients in confusion.

G. Behold yet another devil whom the ancients worshipped, named Tlaloc, or Tlaloque. To him was attributed the rain. They said, "These make trees, grasses, and indeed all our sustenance sprout, bloom, grow." Also to the Tlalocs were attributed drownings, thunderbolts. For the sake of these devils the ancients celebrated a feast day in [the month of] Quauitl eua or Atl caualo, when the new year's ceremony was performed. On their feast day, many small children, called *tlacateteuhti,* were slain on the mountain tops — those who had two cowlicks in the hair, whose day-signs were good. And also they were sought out, bought. It was said that they were most precious blood-offerings.

This was a very great and very fearful sin which the ancients committed for the sake of the devils, the demons, the evil spirits — these Tlalocs. They thought[169] that these gave rain and all our sustenance. Thus were the ancients greatly in confusion, and greatly they offended God. For, indeed, only He Himself giveth all of us men on earth this rain, wherewith is made all our sustenance. For thus is the word of God; behold, *Dabo vobis pluvias, temporibus suis, et terra germinabit germen suum: et pomis arbores replebuntur. Leviticus,* 26. Our Lord God speaketh; he saith, "I shall give you rain, each year, in its good time (if you will live by My com-

ilhujcac: in iquac nemja tlalticpac, iaoiutl qujiolitiaia, iehoatl qujiolitiaia in teuhtli, in tlaçolli, cococ, teupouhqui tepan qujchioaia, tetzalan tenepantla, moquetzaia: ipampa y, moteneoa necoc iautl, teca maujltiaia, tequequeloaia: moteneoa ehecatl, tlaioalli. Jnin tlaueliloc tezcatlipuca, ticmati ca iehoatl in lucifer, in vei diablo, in vmpa ilhujcatl itic, vel iancujcan oqujpeoalti, in iaujutl in tecuculiliztli, in teuhtli, in tlaçolli: vmpa oaltotococ, vmpa oalvetz. Auh in nican tlalticpac teiztlacaujtinemj, teca mocacaiauhtinemj: ca iuh ca in teutlatolli. Factum est prelium magnũ in celo, apoc. 12. quitoznequj, vei iaoiutl, omuchiuh yn ilhujcatl ytic: oqujpeoalti in lucifer: in iehoatl tezcatlipuca, titlacaoa, vei diablo: iehoatl qujmoteutitiaque, in veuetque: yoan qujlhujqujxtiliaia, yn iquac toxcatl: yoan qujmjctiaia yn jxiptla, yn qujtocaiotiaia titlacahoan, ic cenca omotlapololtique in veuetque.

G. Jzcatquj yn oc no ce diablo, qujmoteutitiaque in ueuetque, yn jtoca tlaloc, anoço tlaloque: itech tlamjloia in qujiaujtl: qujtoque. Ca iehoãtin, qujxoaltiaia, qujcueponaltia quizcaltiaia in quaujtl, in çacatl: auh in ie muchi tonacaiutl. No yoan yntech tlamjloia in tlalloque, in teilaqujliztli, tlavitequjliztli: ipampa ynin diablome, qujmilhujqujstiliaia, yn ipan quavitl eoa, anoço atl caoalo in veuetque, in iquac xiuhtzitzqujloia: in ipam imilhujuh, tepeticpac mjctiloia, mjequintin pipiltzitzinti, in moteneoaia tlacateteuhti, in iehoantin yn ontecuezcomeque, in qualli intonal: no yoan temoloia, patiutiloia: mjtooaia, ca iehoantin vel tlaçonextlaoalti.

Jnjn ca cenca vey, yoan cenca temamauhti tlatlaculli, in qujchioaia in veuetque, yn jmpampa diablome, in tzitzitzimj, in culeleti: in iehoan tlaloque, momotia ca iehoanti qujtemaca, in qujaujtl: yoan in isqujch tonacaiutl: ic cenca omotlapololtique in veuetque, yoan cenca, oqujmoiolitlacalhuique yn dios: ca çã vel izeltzin techmomaqujlia, in tisqujchti cemanaoac titlaca in iehoatl, qujavitl, ynjc muchioa yn isqujch tonacajutl: ca iuh ca in teutlatolli, izcatquj. Dabo vobis pluujas, temporibus sujs, et terra germjnabjt germen suum: et pomjs arbores replebuntur. leujtici. 26. Motlatoltia in totecujo dios, qujmitalhuja. Namechnomaqujliz in qujavitl, in cecexiuh-

169. Read *momatia.*

mandments, if you do nothing idolatrous). And at My word the earth will sprout, will bear fruit. And at My word the fruit trees will form much fruit, will greatly increase." Your forefathers knew nothing, they heard nothing of the word of God. Thus did the devils, the true adversaries of us, the people who live on earth, trick them.

tica, yn imonecian (intla uel anqujmonemiliztizque notenaoatil, intlacatle tlateutoqujliztli, anqujchioazque), auh in tlalticpactli notencopa tlaxoaltiz, tlatlaaquillotiz: auh in xochiqualquaujtl, notencopa cenca moxochiquallotiz, cenca tlaaquiz. Jn amoculhoan, amo qujmattiaque atle oqujcactiaque, in teutlatolli: ic cenca inca omocacaiauhque in diablome, in vel toiaoan, in tlalticpac titlaca.

A. Behold how the word of God is, by which are shamed the idolaters: *Incommunicabile nomen lapidibus et lignis imposuerunt. Wisdom*, 14. That is, "So much were the idolaters in confusion that they placed the name of God on stone and wood; they worshipped stone and wood. The [name] God is exclusive to Him Himself, God the Creator through Whom there is life." But the blind idolaters gave the name to stone; they said, "Thou art my god." To wood they said, "Thou art my god, thou art my lord." Also were the idolaters much to be abhorred [because] they placed the name of God, through Whom there is life, upon men, upon women, who were mortals, whose lives were evil, whose hearts were evil. This is the great sin, idolatry, the doing of your fathers, your grandparents, the ancients. Behold their confusion.

A. Jzcatquj in iuh ca teutlatolli, ynic pinauhtilo in tlateutocanjme. Jncõmunjcabile, nomen lapidibus, et lignis inposuerunt: Sapientie 14, q. n. Jn tlateutocanjme ynjc cenca omotlapololtique, in teutocaitl, ytech oqujtlalique, in tetl yoan in quavitl: qujteutocaque in tetl, yoã in quavitl: in teotl, çan vel izeltzin yneixcaujlaxcatzin, in dios in teiocuianj, yn jpalnemoanj. Auh yn jxpopoiome, in tlateutocanjme, qujtocaiotique, in tetl, qujlhujque: ca tinoteouh, qujlhujque, in quaujtl, ca tinoteouh, tinotlatocauh. No yoan in cẽca tlaelittalonj, in tlateutocanjme: yn jtocatzin dios ipalnemoanj, intech oqujtlalique, yn oqujchti, yn cioa: in miqujnj, in palanjnj, yn amo qualli innemiliz, yn amo qualli iniollo. Jnjn ca tetzauhtlatlaculli, in tlateutoqujliztli, yn jntlachioal yn amotahoan, yn amoculhoan, in veuetque: izcatquj yn jnnetlapololtiliz.

B. The ancients worshipped Quetzalcoatl, who was ruler at Tula. And you named him Topiltzin. He was a common man; he was mortal. He died; his body corrupted. He is no god. And although a man of saintly life, who performed penances, he should not have been worshipped. What he did which was like miracles we know he did only through the command of the devil. He is a friend of the devils. Therefore he must needs be abhorred, abominated. Our Lord God hath thrust him into the land of the dead. The ancients went on to say that Quetzalcoatl went to Tlapallan; [that] yet he will return. He is still expected. This is not true; it is falsehood. His body died; here on earth it became dust, it became filth. And his soul our Lord God damned and thrust into the land of the dead. There it is. It will forever suffer in the flames.

B. Jn iehoantin in veuetque, oqujteutocaque in quetzalcoatl, in tollan tlatoanj catca: yoan anqujtocaiotiaia, Topiltzin. Jnin ca maceoalli, ca mjqujni, ca omjc, ca opalan yn jnacaio, ca amo teutl: auh maciuj in iecnemjlize in tlamaceoaia, ca amo qujmoteutizquja: in tlein oqujchiuh, iuhqujnma tlamauiçolli, ticmati ca çan tlacateculotlatoltica oqujchiuh: ca imjcniuh in tlatlacateculo, ic monequj telchioaloz, tlaelittaloz: ca mjctlan oqujmotlaxili in totecujo dios: qujtotiaque in veuetque, ca tlapallan ia in quetzalcoatl, oc vallaz oc chielo: injn ca amo nelli, ca iztlacatlatolli: ca omjc yn jnacaio, nican tlalticpac otlaltic, otlaçoltic: auh yn janjma, oqujmotlatzontequjlili yn totecujo dios, mjctlan, qujmotlaxili, vmpa ca, cemjcac tleco tlaihiiouiz.

C. Behold another confusion of your forefathers. They worshipped a devil in the guise of a woman, named Ciuacoatl. When he appeared before men, it was as a woman that he appeared. She terrified men; she frightened. To her were attributed poverty, misery, the digging-stick, the tump-line, weeping.

C. Jzcatquj, yn oc centlamantli ynnetlapololtiliz yn amoculhoan, ca oqujmoteutique in diablo, yn ipã mixeoa cioatl, yn jtoca cioacoatl. Jnjn yn iquac motenestiliaia, iuhq'nma cioatl, ynjc necia: teiçaviaia, tlamauhtiaia, ytech tlamjloia, injc iehoatl qujtemacaia, in netolinjliztli, yn jcnoiutl, in victli in mecapalli, in

And because of this they celebrated her feast day. They laid offerings before her, they slew victims before her, that her anger, her fury, might not fall upon [them]. This which your forefathers thus lived doing was a very great confusion. They knew not that only He alone through Whom there is life watcheth over men, defendeth men. And the devil in no way harmeth the believers in God who have faith in Him. For so is the word of God: *Quoniam in me sperabit, liberabo eum, protegam eum: quoniam cognovit nomen meum, clamavit ad me, et ego exaudiam eum, cum ipso sum in tribulatione, eripiam eum et glorificabo eum. Ps.* 90. That is, God saith, "He who will believe in Me and have faith in Me I shall aid, I shall take his side. For he knew My name. He will cry out to Me; I shall hear him with favor, I shall comfort him. When he is in anguish, I shall deliver him; I shall aid him." This is plain, that only our Lord God Himself customarily aideth men, customarily defendeth men. And it is required that only He Himself be called upon, be supplicated, when anything afflicteth us.

D. In many other ways the devils, the demons, tricked the ancients. They made them believe in certain goddesses; they paid attention to them, and for their sake celebrated feast days for them, and laid offerings before them, and slew victims.

One was named Chicome coatl. To her was attributed the maize — whatsoever was the means of life of the common folk. A second was Teteo innan, or Tlalli iyollo; and she was also known as Toci. The ancients held that this one gave birth to the gods, whence came men on earth. Hence was she named "our grandmother" [Toci]. This Teteo innan the physicians served — the leeches, those who purged one, those who cured one's eyes; and the women, midwives, those who administered sedatives at childbirth, those who induced abortions, soothsayers, casters of auguries by looking upon the water, by scattering grains of maize, by using knotted cords, who removed foreign objects from the body, who removed worms from the teeth, from the eyes. Also those who had sweat-houses prayed to her. Because of this they set up her image in the front of the sweat-house, and they gave her the name, "Grandmother of the Baths." And all of those celebrated her feast day each year; they laid offerings before her; they slew victims before her.

choquiztli. Auh yn ipampa hi, qujlhujqujxtiliaia: ixpan tlamanaia, ixpan tlamjctiaia, ynjc amo ipan vechoaz in iqualan, yn jtlauel. Jnin iuh qujchiuhtinenca, yn amoculhoan, cenca vei netlapololtiliztli: amo qujmatia, ca çan vel izeltzin in ipalnemoanj totecujo dios, motepielia, motemanavilia: auh in diablo, njman aquen qujnchioaz yn itlaneltocacaoan in dios, yn jtetzinco motemachia, ca iuh ca yn teutlatolli. Quonjam in me sperabit, liberabo eum, protegam eum: quonjam cognoujt nomen meum: clamabit ad me, et ego exaudiam eum, cum ipso sum in tribulatione eripiam eum, et glorificabo eum. psal. 90. qujtoznequj: Motlatoltia yn dios. Jn aquin nechneltocaz, yoan notech motemachiz, njcpaleuiz, ipan njnilacatzoz: ipampa ca oqujxima, in notocatzin: nechmotzatziliz, nictlavelcaqujliz, niciollaliz, yn iquac motequipachoz, njcmaqujxtiz, nicpaleuiz. Jnjn ca vel ic neci, ca çan izeltzin totecujo dios, motepaleujlianj, motemanavilianj: auh ca monequj, çan vel izeltzin notzaloz, tlatlauhtiloz; in iquac itla techtequjpachoa.

D. Oc miec tlamantli, ynic inca mocacaiauhque in veuetque in diablome, in tzitzitzimj, oqujntlaneltoqujtique: ca cequjntin cioateteu inpan qujnmatia: auh yn jpampa y, qujmilhujqujxtiliaia, yoan ymjxpan tlamanaia, yoan tlamjctiaia.

Ce ytoca chicume coatl: in iehoatl in, itech tlamjloia, in tonacaiutl, in çaço tlein, ỹnenca injulca in maceoalti: ynic vme teteu innan, anoço tlalli yiollo, no yoan moteneoaia toci: qujtotiaque in veuetque, ca in iehoatl i, oquintlacatili in teteu: ca neci in tlalticpac tlaca, ipampa in moteneoa toci. Jn iehoatl teteu inna, qujtlaieicultiaia yn titici, in teitzminque, yn tetlanoqujlique, teispatique; auh in cioa, in temjxiujtianj, tepillalilianj, tetlatlaxilianj, tlapouhque, atlan teittanj, tlaulchaiauhque, mecatlapouhque, tetlacujcujlique, tetlanocujlanque, teixocujlanque. No qujtlatlauhtiaia in temazcaleque: ipampa y, qujtlalia yn ixiptla, yn ixquac in temazcalli: yoan qujtocaiotiaia, temazcalteci. Auh yn jsqujchtin hi, qujlhujqujxtiliaia, cecexiujtl, ispan tlamanaia, ispan tlamjctiaia.

E. Yet another woman they worshipped; she was called Tzapotlan tenan. To her was attributed turpentine unguent, and they said that she aided those with itch of the head, she applied unguent to the throat of those who were hoarse. Those applied it to themselves who had head sores, who had pimples on the head, who had cracks on the feet, cracked lips, chapped faces, and jigger fleas; [also] the tortilla-sickness.[170] The turpentine unguent, or turpentine liquid, was required for indeed many purposes. This the ancients thus told. They only lied; they only thus tricked men.

E. Oc no ce cioatl, qujmoteutiaia itoca tzaputla tena: itech tlamiloia in vxitl, yoan qujtoaia ca qujnpaleujaia in quaxocociuj, in tozcamjiaoaciuj, qujntozcavxiuja, in chaquachiuj, in quaçaoati, in xutzaianj, in tentzaianj, yn isteteçonauj, yn jcxitzaianj: yoan in qualocatl, intech motlalia, in tlaxcaliciuiztli. Jn vxitl, yn anoçe vxiatl, vel mjeccan moneq', ynjn iuh qujtotiaque in veuetque, ca çã oiztlacatiaque, çan ic teca omocacaiauhque.

And when her feast day was celebrated, the turpentine unguent merchants bought for themselves and slew a slave. They made her representation of amaranth seed dough. There were many other ways by which they paid honor to this Tzapotlan tenan.

Auh yn iquac ilhujqujstililoia, in vxinamacaque, motlacacoujaia, tlacamictiaia, qujtzoallotiaia in jxiptla: oc mjec tlamantli, ynjc qujmauiztiliaia y, in iehoatl tzaputla tena.

F. Still another goddess whom your forefathers worshipped was named Chalchiuhtli icue. They said she was among the Tlalocs; she was their elder sister. It was said that she drowned people, plunged them into the water, she drowned them, she sank them. Hence she greatly terrified; she was feared. The water-merchants and the water folk celebrated her feast day, and before her they laid offerings and slew victims. With many such acts they honored her; it was in vain, it was only their confusion.

F. Oc no ce ciuateutl, oqujmoteutitiaque in amoculhoan, yn jtoca chalchiuhtli ycue: qujtoaia, invam pouj, inveltiuh in tlaloque: qujlmach teatoctiaia, teatlanmjctiaia, tepolactiaia: ic cenca tlamauhtiaia ymacaxoia. Qujlhujqujstiliaia yn anamacaque, yoan atlaca: yoã ixpan tlamanaia, yoan tlamictiaia: mjec tlamantli ynjc qujmauiztiliaia, in çan nen, in çan innetlapololtilizpã.

Still other evil women your fathers, your grandfathers worshipped. [One] was named Tlaçolteotl, to whom were attributed vice, filth. It is said that four women arose. The first was named Tiacapan, the second was named Teicu, the third was named Tlaco, the fourth was named Xocotzin. These four women were looked upon as god[desses]. They were called goddesses of filth [*tlaçolteteo*]. From these, the names of the goddesses of filth, your young girls have taken their names — some have been named Tiacapan, some Teicu, some Tlaco, some Xocotzin. This is idolatry. It is necessary that it cease, that it be abhorred. Your fathers, your grandfathers worshipped these harlots, and before them slew victims, before them laid offerings.

Oc no cequjntin, in cioatlaueliloque in qujnteutocatiaque yn amotahoan,yn amoculhoan, yn itoca tlaçulteutl: ytech tlamjloia, in teuhtli, in tlaçulli: qujl naujntin eoa cioa: injc ce, ytoca tiacapan, ynjc vme, itoca teicui, inic ey, itoca tlacu, ynic nauj ytoca xocutzi. Jn iehoan hi, in navinti cioa impam machoia teteu: in iehoantin y motocaiotia tlaçulteteu: yn intech in yn intoca, in tlaçulteteu, qujcuj yn jntoca yn amochpuchoan cequjntin qujmotocaiotia, tiacapan, cequjntin teicuj, cequjntin tlacu, cequjnti xucutzin. Jnjn ca tlateutoqujliztli, ca monequj caoaloz, tlaelittaloz: in iehoantin in in naujanjme, qujnmoteutitiaque yn amotahoan, yn amoculhoan: yoan ymjxpan tlamjctiaia, ymixpan tlamanaia.

G. The devil blinded the ancients with another confusion. He caused them to believe in the women who died in childbirth who, they said, became god-

G. Oc no centlamantli, netlapololtiliztli ic oqujmixpupuiotili in diablo in veuetque, oqujntlaneltoqujti: in iehoantin in mocioaquetzque, qujtoaia mo-

170. See n. 51, *supra*.

desses. They named them Ciuateteo, Ciuapipiltin. It was an attribute of theirs, it was said, that they were angered by men; they tricked men. When someone was under their spell, he was possessed, his mouth was twisted, his face contorted, he lacked use of a hand, his feet were misshapen, his feet were deadened, his hand trembled, he foamed at the mouth. So it was said that they had met, contended, with the Ciuapipiltin. For this reason they were greatly revered; they were worshipped. In their houses, at crossroads, gifts were set out before them; their feast day was celebrated. Many things they thus offered them on their feast day. This which your forefathers proceeded to do, in worshipping many women, was indeed a confusion and laughable. Much were they thereby shamed. This, verily, all the word of God refuteth.

teucuepa, qujntocaiotique, cioateteu, cioapipilti. Jntech tlamiloia, qujlmach tetlaueliaia, teca mocacaiaoaia, injc aca itech qujneoaia, in tlavelilocatia, tennecujliuja, isnecujliuja, matzicuiliujaia, icxicupichauja: icximjmjquja, momacuecuetzaia, tēqualacqujçaia: ic mjtoaia ca omotenamjcti, ipan oquizque in cioapipilti: in ipampa hi cenca imacaxoia, neteutiloia, in chachan in vmaxac, imixpan tlamanaloia: ilhujqujxtililoia, mjec tlamantli ic qujntlamanjliaia, yn imjlhujuh ipan. Jnjn in qujchiuhtiaque, yn amoculhoan, injc q'nmoteutiaia, mjequjnti cioa, vel tetlapololti, yoan teuetzqujti, cenca ic omopinauhtique: injn ca uel qujtlauelnamjquj yn isqujch teutlatolli.

A. The ancients worshipped many more gods whom they did not consider equal to those [already] mentioned. But of these, one, the fire, was everywhere worshipped. They named him Xiuhtecutli. And they also named him Ixcoçauhqui, and also Cueçaltzin, and Ueue teotl, and Tota. He was thought a god because he burned one, he consumed one, he singed one. And many other things were his office. The feast day of this Xiuhtecutli was observed in [the month of] Izcalli. And before him victims were slain, gifts were laid; before him there was dancing. And many other things were done because of the honors paid this Ixcoçauhqui. This your forefathers, the ancient, lived doing. Thus it clearly appeareth that their blindness was very great. For they worshipped that which seeth not, nor heareth, nor liveth; which is only a creature of God — a gift made for us that it may serve us. Hence it is required that our Lord God be honored, praised, served, for what He hath given unto us.

A. Oc no mjequjnti teteu, oqujnmoteutitiaque in veuetque, yn amo qujnneneujlia yn omoteneuhque: auh ceme iehoan in, in iehoatl in tletl, in vel noujian neteutiloc, oqujtocaiotique xiuhtecutli, no yoã oqujtocaiotique, iscuçauhquj, no yoan cueçaltzin, yoan veueteutl, yoan tota: Jnin teutl ipan machoia, iehica ca tetlatia, tepaloa, techichinoa: yoan oc cequj miec tlamantli itequjo. Jnjn xiuhtecutli ilhujqujstililoia yn ipan izcalli: yoã yispan tlamictiloia, tlamanaloia, ispan netotiloia. Auh oc cequj mjec tlamãtli, muchioaia, ipampa yn jmauiztililoca, in iscuçauhquj: ynjn yn iuh quichiuhtinenca, yn amoculhoan in veuetque: ic vel neci ca cenca vey, yn jmjxpupuiotiliz: ca qujmoteutiaia yn amo tlachia, yn amo tlacaquj, yn amo iuli, in çan itlachioaltzin dios: tonemac omuchiuh, ynjc techtlaiecultiz: ypampa iehoatl monequj mauiztililoz, iecteneoaloz, tlaiecultiloz, yn otechmomaqujlitzino in totecujo dios.

B. Still another devil whom the ancients worshipped they named Ixtlilton and Xochipilli.[171] They said that when there was fasting, if one of us men lay with a woman, or a woman with a man, they said they brought to naught their fasting through sin. Wherefore he would visit them with piles, with hemorrhoids, suppurating genitals, disease of the groin, wherefore they made vows to him in order to quiet, to remove the sickness. For this reason they

B. Oc no ce diablo qujmoteutitiaque, in veuetque, in qujtocaiotique, istlilton, yoan xuchipilli: ynjn qujtoaia, yn jquac neçavililoia: intla aca toq'chti ipan cioacuchiz, anoço cioatl ipan oquichcuchiz, qujtoaia, qujtlaçolmjctiaia yn ineçaoaliz: ic tetech qujtlaliaia, in suchiciuiztli, in menexoaliztli, in tlapalanaltiliztli, in quexiliujliztli. Jn ipampa hi, yujc nenetoltiloia, ynic qujceuiz, ynjc qujquaniz in cuculiztli: ipampa qujlhujq'xtiliaia, qujneçaujliaia, qujtlamanjliaia.

171. The incorrect pairing of Ixtlilton and Xochipilli is in the Nahuatl text. The Spanish text is correct.

celebrated his feast day, they mourned for him, they offered him gifts. This was a great folly of the ancients, this which they thus lived doing on his account; for they kept not, they knew not the word of God. But now, know well that only He alone, the true God, is the healer of men, the giver of life to men. There is no other. When something befalleth us — pain, affliction — He alone may be sought, prayed to, as is the word of God, as hath been said above.

Jnjn ca vey, yn innetlapololtiliz in veuetque, yn ipampa iuhquj qujchiuhtinenca: ca atle qujpiaia, atle qujmatia, in teutlatolli. Auh in axcan, ma uel xicmatican, çan vel izeltzin, izel teutl dios, motepatilianj, moteiolitilianj, aiac oc ce: in jquac itla topan muchioa, in tecoco, in tetolinj, çan vel izeltzin, tlatlauhtiloz, temuloz, iuh ca in teutlatolli, in tlacpac omjto.

C. Yet another devil whom the ancients worshipped was named Omacatl. They said that feasts, invitations to feasts, gatherings of kinsfolk were his introduction. To one's house was brought, there to be paid honor, his representation. Yet many more things your forefathers went on to say of him, went on to ascribe to him in their childishness, their puerility, which were lies, laughable, in no way to be believed.

Likewise one Ixtlilton or Tlaltetecuin was a god of the ancients. There was his black water. And also it was said that it was his office to tap it, to offer the new wine. Many other things were ascribed to him, and they did many things as recreation [when] they took Ixtlilton to their homes. Thus it appeareth that the ancients are to be wept for, to be reproached to tears, because they believed childish things, puerile things, unbelievable things.

C. Oc no ce diablo qujmoteutiaia, in veuetque, yn itoca omacatl, in qujtoaia ca iehoatl ymactia in covaiutl, in tecoanotzaliztli, yn jnnecentlaliliz in tevaniolque: techan vicoia, vmpa mauiztililoia in ixiptla: oc cenca miec tlamantli, itech oqujtotiaque, ytech oqujtlamjtiaque, in amoculhoã, in cucuneiutl, in pipillutl, in iztlacatlatolli: in teuetzqujti, in njman amo neltoconj.

Çan no iehoatl istlilton, anoço tlaltetecujn, inteouh catca in veuetque: vncatca yn jtlilauh: no yoan qujlmach itequjuh, tlaiacaxaputlaia, vitzmanaia: oc no mjec tlamantli, itech tlamjloia: yoan mjec tlamantli, neaviltiliztli, in qujchioaia, yn jnchã, qujvicaia, yn istlilton; ic neci ca cenca techoctique, vel tetozqujtenque, in vevetque: iehica ca qujneltocaia, yn amo neltoconj, in cucunejutl, im pipillutl.

D. Still another devil who was a god of the ancients was named Opochtli. They said he was the god of the water folk. Thus they said that of his originating were the net, the atlatl, the trident, the boating pole, the rope for snaring. And when his feast day was celebrated, many were the gifts which they laid before him. And many were the things which they did before him, these water folk whom the devil thus deluded. Thus did they greatly offend our Lord God.

Still another devil did the ancient ones worship, named Totec, or Xipe. It was said that his office was to wound men with blisters, festering, pimples, eye pains, watering of the eyes, festering about the eyelashes, lice about the eyes, opacity, cataracts, glazing of the eyes. Whosoever of us men this befell — this sickness — it was said, vowed that he would wear the skin of Totec. This was a great confusion, a great blindness which your forefathers left to you.

D. Oc no ce diablo inteouh catca in veuetque, yn jtoca opuchtli: qujtoque ca inteouh, yn atlaca, iuh qujtoaia ca iehoatl itlatzintil, in matlatl, yn atlatl, in mjnacachalli, ỹ aujctli, in tzonvaztli. Auh yn iquac ilhujqujstililoia, miec tlamantli in ventli, in jspan qujmanaia: yoan oc mjec tlamãtli ixpan qujchioaia, yn atlaca, in iuh qujmiztlacauj in diablo: ic cenca oqujmoiolitlacalhujque in totecujo dios.

Oc no ce diablo, oqujmoteutitiaque in veuetque, yn jtoca totec, anoço xipe: qujl itequjuh catca, ic temotlaia in totomonjliztli, papalanjliztli, çaçaoatiliztli, iscocoliztli, ischichitinaliztli, istenpipixqujliztli, istamaçoliciuiztli, isaiauhpachiujliztli, istotoliciuiztli, istezcaiciuiztli: in aq'n ipan muchioaia yn, in cocoliztli toqujchtin, iujcpa mjtoaia, monetoltiaia, ynjc vmmaquiz yeoaio totec. Jnjn ca vei netlapololtiliztli, vey ispupuiotiliztli, yn amotech qujcauhtiaque, yn

Unhappy are they; especially unhappy are they now who perchance still remember it.

amoculhoan: ointlaveliltic, oc cēca ointlaueliltic, yn axcan, yn açoc qujlnamiquj.

E. Still another devil whom the ancient ones worshipped was named Yiacatecutli and Yacacoliuhqui. It was said that he was the god of the merchants. Each year the merchants celebrated his feast day. They slew many slaves before him, and in many ways they thus paid him honor. Unhappy are they who devised this; especially unhappy are those who even now remember it.

E. Oc no ce diablo, oqujmoteutitiaque yn veuetque, yn jtoca yiacatecutli, yoan iacaculiuhquj: qujl inteouh in puchteca, cecexiuhtica, qujlhujquistiliaia, in puchteca: mjequjntin tlatlacuti, ispan qujmjctiaia: yoan mjec tlamantli, ynjc qujmaviztiliaia, ointlaueliltic, in iehoantin, in qujiocuxtiaque hi, oc cenca ointlaveliltic, yn noma qujlnamjquj.

F. Yet another devil whom the ancients worshipped was named Napa tecutli. It was said that he was god of the makers of reed mats, of coarse reed mats. Likewise they said that he caused to sprout the reeds for mats, the white reeds, the cylindrical reeds, etc. And each year the mat-makers, the makers of round reed mats, the makers of coarse reed mats celebrated his feast day. And when his feast day came, his old men did much wickedness. Unhappy are they alone who thus went doing this. Twenty score times unhappy are those who even now remember it. For the devil will carry off their souls.

F. Oc no ce diablo oqujmoteutitiaque, in veuetque, yn itoca nappa tecutli: qujl ynteouh in petlachiuhque, yoan in tlacuechiuhque. No qujtoaia ca iehoatl, qujxoaltiaia, in petlatolin, yn aztapili, yn tolmjmjlli, etc. Auh cexiuhtica qujlhujqujxtiliaia, in petlachiuhque, in tolcuechiuhque, in tlacuechiuhque: auh yn iquac ynilhujuh quiçaia, yn iehoantin yn jveueiovan, cenca mjec tlamantli tlavelilocaiutl, qujchioaia. Ocelintlaveliltic, yn iuh qujchiuhtiaque hi: o centzompa yn tlaveliltic intla cequjnti noma qujlnamiquj, ca diablo qujnvicaz yn jmanjma.

G. Another devil whom the ancients worshipped was one whose name was Tezcatzoncatl. It was said that he made the wine; it was said that it was of his invention. Many others were his friends, were devils like him. This same wine was their office. For all there was worshipping, there was celebration of feast days, there was giving of service because of their wickedness — for they cast men from crags, they strangled them, they slew them. Especially did those who scraped the maguey plant do many things whereby they served him. Unhappy are they who lived so doing; especially unhappy if some even now live so doing or live remembering it. For the devil will carry off their souls.

G. Oc no ce diablo, qujmoteutitiaque in veuetque, yn jtoca catca tezcatzoncatl: qujl qujchiuh yn vctli, qujl itlanextil, oc no mjequjnti yn jcnioan, yn jtlacateculopoa: çan no iehoatl yn vctli yn intequjuh catca. Ca muchinti neteutiloia, ilhujqujstililoia, tlaiecultiloia, ypampa yn jntlavelilocaio, ynjc tetepexiujaia, tequechmecanjaia, temjctiaia: oc cenca iehoanti yn tlachicque, mjec tlamantli, qujchioaia ynjc qujntlaiecultiaia. Ointlaueliltic, yn juh qujchiuhtinenca, oc cenca ointlaveliltic, intla cequjntin noma iuh qujchiuhtinemj, yn anoço qujlnamjctinemj: ca diablo qujnvicaz yn jmanjma.

A. There was still another confusion which your forefathers went leaving to you. For they went on to say that the mountains were gods; wherefore they formed mountain [figures], and they called their representations Tepictoton. And they made vows to them — those with the palsy — that they would form them, etc. And when they had formed them, then they laid offerings before them, they sang before them, they did many things in their presence in order to pay them honor. Greatly were they in confusion if not completely besotted. And today it is not completely uprooted; even now some pay their debts on

A. Oc no centlamantli netlapololtiliztli, amotech qujcauhtiaque, yn amoculhoã: ca oqujtotiaque, in tetepe ca teteu: ipãpa quinpiquja in tetepe. Auh yn jmixiptlavan, qujntocaiotiaia tepictoton: yoan ynvic monetoltiaia, in coaciuja, ynjc tepiquizque, etc. Auh yn oqujnpicque, njman, imixpan tlamanaia, ymjxpan cujcujcaia, mjec tlamantli, ymjxpan qujchioaia; ynjc qujnmaviztiliaia: vel motlapololtiaia in maca çan tlavancapupul. Auh yn axcan ca aiamo cempoliuj, noma cequjnti, moxtlaoa tepeticpac: auh ynjn ca vei tlatlaculli, vey yiolitlaculoca yn dios, vey eregia, ca tetzauhtlatlaculli.

mountain tops. But this is a great sin, a great offense to God, a great heresy. It is an abominable sin.

B. Behold also [what] the ancients did in order to pay honor to the mountains: they made Tepicme like men. Hence they placed masks on them. And this the *tlamacazque*, the priests of Tlaloc, did. And when they made these, the common folk, those who had made vows, laid offerings before them; in their presence they ate, they drank, they danced. And when their feast day came, they divided the Tepicme among themselves and ate them. This which your forefathers did was childish; it was puerile.

C. Many other things of confusion did your forefathers do. And your fathers, your grandfathers worshipped very many other gods, without number, whom no one can record, and whom also no one can count, there were so many.

B. Jzcatquj no qujchioaia, yn veuetque, ynjc qujnmauiztiliaia in tetepe: qujnchioaia tepicme, iuhqujnma titlaca, ynjc qujnxaiacatiaia: auh ynjn, iehoantin qujchioaia, in tlamacazque, yn jntlamacazcaoan tlaloque. Auh yn jquac ie oqujnchiuhque: in iehoantin in maceoalti, yn netoleque ymixpan tlamanaia, ymjxpan tlaquaia, atlia, mjtotiaia. Auh yn jquac oquiz ilhujtl, qujnmococotinjaia yn tepicme: yoan qujnquaia. Ynjn iuh qujchioaia, yn amoculhoã ca cocunejutl, ca pipillutl.

C. Oc no mjec tlamantli, netlapololtiliztli oqujchiuhtiaque, yn amoculhoan: yoan oc cenca mjequjnti, yn amo çan tlapoalti in teteu in oqujnmoteutique, in amotahoan, yn amoculhoan, in aiac vel qujcujloz: yoan in anoiac vel qujnpoaz, ynjc cenca mjequjnti.

* * *

Let him who readeth this understand it well.

Whosoever thou art who readest the words which have been said above, which have been written, look thou well, know them well. My command is being made in the presence of God, that thou shalt speak if thou knowest if any live practising or if anywhere is practised the idolatry spoken of above. Thou shalt then expose it before the justice of the Holy Church, the priests, or the justice of the Royal Audiencia, the *alguaciles*, especially the *padres*, not only as a confession [but] verily as an accusation. And thou shalt tell this speedily; thou shalt not delay, neither shalt thou have fear. Thou shalt indeed expose to the priest what thou hast thus heard, what thou hast thus seen. If any know of, if they witness idolatry, if they wish not to tell of it, if they wish not to expose it before the priest, they are idolaters, they are devils, our Lord God's foes.

* * *

Ma uel qujcaquj, in qujpoaz hi.

In ac tehoatl, in ticpoaz in, in tlatolli in tlacpac omjto, yn omjcujlo, cenca tle ticmati: vel xicmati, ca monahoatil muchiuhtica, yn jspantzinco in dios, injc titlatoz, intla ticmati, intla aca qujchiuhtinemj, anoço canapa muchiva, yn omjto tlateutoqujliztli: njman tiqujspantiliz, yn jiusticia in sancta yglesia, in teupisque: yn anoço yiusticia in audientia real: in topileque, oc cenca iehoantin in padreme: amo çan neiolmelaoalizpan, vel neteilhujlizpan. Auh ynjn iciuhca tiqujtoz: amo ticvecaoaz, amono timomauhtiz: vel tiqujspantiliz in teupisquj, yn juh otiqujttac, yn juh oticcac. Jn aqujque yntla qujmati, intla oqujttaque, in tlateutoqujliztli, yn amo qujtoznequj, yn amo qujspantiliznequj: in teupisquj: ca tlateutocanjme, ca diablome, yiauoan in totecujo dios.

* * *

Behold the words of sorrow, the words of pity, which [the author] hath set on paper; how he crieth out greatly. He prayeth to God; he sayeth:

* * *

Jzca in ichoquiztlatol, yn jtlaocullatol, in amatl oqujtlali: inic cenca tzatzi, in qujmotlatlauhtilia dios, qujtoa.

* * *

Alas, my heart weepeth exceedingly, my tears are indeed gathered upon my face. Like hailstones my tears fall as I think upon the many kinds of lies by

Iioiave, cenca chocan noiollo, vel njxaio njxtlan moteteca: iuhqujn teciujtl pixavi njxaio, ynjc niqujlnamjquj, ca cenca mjec tlamantli, iztlacatlatolli, ynjc

which the people here in New Spain were led into error — not for only four hundred years, not for only eight hundred years; for much time in the past.

Alas, my heart suffereth much — it is as if my heart burneth — as I stop to think how great is the hatred of the demon of the air, of Satan, for men. So much he hateth us men on earth. For greatly he acteth with all his power in order to go bringing down us sons of Adam to our ruin, our shame, our degradation. This he hath thus gone bringing to pass through lies, delusion, treachery.

Alas, O Lord God, when I consider Thy commandments, the sternness of Thy divine judgments, much am I afraid, much am I terrified. O Lord God, for all time Satan hath tricked the people of New Spain. Why hast Thou not known them? For very many are his lies, the darkness, which he hath spewed over them. Thus hath this Satan offended Thee, thus hath he disrespected Thee. And he hath ill-used, greatly shamed all us men on earth. And I am greatly angered because Satan hath so done. Wherefore I humbly pray to Thee, O our Lord: seize, imprison Satan, that he may nevermore thus act. And also I humbly pray to Thee that Thou wilt offer the natives Thy grace, that Thou wilt offer them Thy great, divine light, the like of which hath not been, so great have been sin [and] darkness.

iztlacaviloque, in nican nueua españa tlaca: ca amo çan centzonxiujtl, ca amo çan vntzonxiujtl, ca cenca ie uecauh.

Jioiaue, cenca noiollo toneoa, vel iuhqujn tlatla noiollo: injc niqujlnamjctimotlalia, yn quenjn cenca vei, yn jtecuculiliz in tzitzimjtl, in satanas: injc techcuculia, yn tlalticpac titlaca: iehica vel yiollocopa, vel ixqujch ytlapal qujchioa, ynjc qujtemotinemj, yn topoliujliz, in totlanjtlaçaloca, yn totelchioaloca, yn tipilhoã Adan: injn ca teiztlacaujliztica, teca necaiavaliztica, teichtacamjctiliztica, yn iuh qujchiuhtinemj.

Jioiaue, totecujoe, diose, yn jquac niqujtztimotlalia, in motlatlaliltzin, yn vuj moteutetlatzontequjlilitzi: ca cenca ninomauhtia, cenca njniçavia: totecujoe, diose, yn jsqujch cavitl, in oic in ca mocacaiauhtinê, in satanas, in nueua españa tlaca: tleica, yn amo tiqujnmocujtitzino? ca cenca mjiec yn jiztlac, yn jtenqualac, in tlaioalli, in jmpãc oqujçotlac: injn ca ic omitzmoiolitlacalujtzino, ic mocpactzinco onẽ yn satanas: auh in timuchinti in cemanaoac titlaca, cenca otechaujlqujxti, cenca otechpinauhti. Auh in nehoatl, ca cenca njqualanj, yn ipampa injc oiuh qujchiuh in satanas: ic cenca nimitznotlatlauhtilia totecujoe: ma xicmolpili, ma xicmocaltzacujli, in satanas, injc aoqujc oc cepa iuhquj qujchioaz. Auh no cenca ic nimitznotlatlauhtilia, ynjc tiqujnmomaqujliz, yn njcan tlaca, yn mograciatzin, tiqujnmomaqujliz, in vei moteutlanetzin, yn amo mach iuhquj catca, in tlatlaculli, in tlaioalli, çan oc cenca ic tlapanauiz.

ADDENDA I *and* II

ADDENDUM I[172]

Amimitl and Atlaua[173]

They were gods of the Chinampaneca of Cuitlauac. For this were they much feared, that these same brought it about that[174] one voided blood, had a bloody excrement, had dysentery; one had colds, a dry cough, a fatal cough, a cold in the head. One went coughing; one coughed.

But as to how they celebrated their feast day, little is known of it here. The Chinampaneca know it.

His array [consisted of] bright red lips — colored lips. And the edges of his eyes were dark; they made the star painting about his face; he had a shield on his forehead. He was striped blue. He had a paper shoulder-sash. He had a paper breech clout. He had white sandals. His shield was half blood-colored; it had feather balls. His staff was the *timetl.*[175]

Amimitl yoã atlavâ

Ynteuvan catca, yn Cuitlauaca, chinãpaneca. Inin uel imacaxoya, ca yevatin q'chiuaya yn iquac aca Eztli quinoq'a tlaelli quitlaça mapiça tlatlaci vacca-tlatlaci. mimiq̃ tlatlaciztli tzompiliui totolcatinemi totolca

Auh ynic q̃milhuiq'xtiliaya amo cenca macho ỹ nicã yeoatin q'mati chinãpaneca

yn inechichival. tenchichiltic. tentlapaltic Auh yxtetlilcomole mizçitlalchiuh yxquatechimale tehxu-uauanq' Amaneapanale Amamaxtle yztaccaque yn ichimal Eztlapanq' yvihteteyo Tymetl yn itopil

172. The Nahuatl text of Addenda I and II is found in Francisco del Paso y Troncoso: *Códice Matritense del Real Palacio,* Vol. VII, pp. 7–8 and pp. 38–40. It appears probable that Sahagún originally intended these accounts to round out the material presented in Book I.

173. Sahagún's heading, *Capitulo decimo,* reads: *"estos dos dioses adoravã los de Cuytlavac y todos los de las chinãpas a estos atribujan q̃ davã y sanavã las camaras de sangre y las otras sin sangre, y la tos y catarro: y los enfermos destas enfermedades los vigilabã y davã ofrendas porq̃ los sanasẽ."* Eduard Seler's translation appears on pp. 31–32 of *Einige Kapitel.*

174. *Ibid.,* p. 31: *"Denn sie machten es"*; reference of *es* remains unclear.

175. The Nahuatl text for Atlaua in *Primeros Memoriales* reads: *"ytlavitimeuh imac icac."* Seler (*Gesammelte Abhandlungen,* Vol. II, p. 485) states: *"Mit den* Chachalmeca *theilt er auch das* tlauitimetl, *'das rothe* timetl,' *das im Buch I kurzweg als* timetl *bezeichnet ist."* Reference is evidently to the forked reed carried in the right hand. Seler (*loc. cit.*) cites the song to Atlaua in Book II of Sahagún and adds: *"Offenbar stellt das* tlauitimetl, *das der Gott in der Hand hält, dieses gespaltene Rohr* (acaxeliui *oder* acatl xeliui) *vor."* See also Sahagún (Garibay ed.), Vol. IV, p. 282, and León-Portilla: *Ritos, sacerdotes y atavíos de los dioses,* p. 240.

ADDENDUM II[176]

Chapter 24. They also considered the sun to be a very important god; but because he is discussed later, in this, the last chapter of the first Book, only a few adages told of this same sun are adduced.

Capitulo 24 tanbiẽ tenjan al sol por dios muy principal y porq' adelante se trata del, en este postrero capitulo deste primero libro solamente se ponẽ algunos adagios contados del mjsmo sol

ADAGES

WHERE THE SUN COMETH, THE WARMTH THEN COMETH; OR WHERE I HAVE NOTED THAT IT GROWETH WARM, THE SUN WILL COME FORTH

That is to say, whatsoever begins, slowly increases. Such is one who gains a livelihood; slowly his goods, his possessions increase. And such is the student; slowly he gains in esteem. Such is the small child; slowly he gains prudence. Thus all which starts is similar. This is not said of wickedness.

NOW THE SUN SHINETH; IT IS LIGHT

That is to say, something new comes to pass. A new law begins. Or the ruler is installed, is selected.

A NEW SUN EMERGETH

It means just the same thing.

HE SETTETH OUT HIS SUN

That is to say, he is married. The woman especially says: "I discover my sun; I set out my sun." The woman says: "Have I perchance [already] come upon my sun?" That is to say, "Have I once before been married?"

WILL PERCHANCE THE TURQUOISE SHIELD APPEAR SHINING? OR: WILL PERCHANCE THE TURQUOISE SHIELD COME TO APPEAR SHINING?

That is to say: That which is good, that which is righteous has vanished; it has forever vanished; it is

ADAGIOS

CAN VITZ TONATIUH NIMÃ TOTONIXTIVITZ ANOÇO CÃ NIQUITAC NIMÃ TOTONIXTIVITZ VALQUIÇAZ TONATIUH.

quitoznequi. In tlein ompeva Çan yvian veixtiuh. In iuhqui motlayecultiani. çã yvian veia in itlatqui yn iaxca. yoã in iuhqui momachtiani çã yvian y vei quimati. Iuhqui ỹ piltõtli çã yviã in ixtlamati. yc mochi iuhqui ỹ tlein ompeva. amo ipã mitoa yn tlavelilocayotl

AXCÃ TONA TLATVI

quitoznequi. hitla yancuic mochiva yancuic tlamanitiliztli õpeva. anoço tlatoanj motlalia. mopepena.

YANCUIC TONATIUH VALMOMANA.

çan no yehoatl qujtoznequi.

CENTETL ITONATIUH QUIVALMANA.

quitoznequi. monamictia. oc cenca yeh in civatl yn quitoa centetl notonatiuh niquitta. centetl notonatiuh niqualmana. quitoa in ciuatl cuix ocẽtetl notonatiuh niquittac. q. n. cuix oceppa nonamicti

CUIX OC CEPPA XIUHCHIMALTONATIMOMANAZ. ANOÇO CUIX OC CEPPA XIUHCHIMALTONATIMOMANAQUIUH.

q. n. yn tlein qualli yn tleĩ yectli opoliuh ocẽmayan poliuh ocẽmayan hitlacauh. In iuhqui haca vei tla-

---

176. See n. 172. Sahagún's heading is written in his hand on the margin. Cf. also Arthur J. O. Anderson and Charles E. Dibble: *Florentine Codex*, Book VII, "The Sun, Moon, and Stars, and the Binding of the Years" (Santa Fe: The School of American Research and The University of Utah, 1953), Chapters 1 and 2.

forever corrupted. It is as [when] some great ruler has died, has vanished, or has been disgraced. It is as [when] a good law has disappeared, or [when] wealth has vanished — or a house.

The *xiuh-* means blue; *chimal-* means shield, that is, round; *tonati-* means the sun; *momanaquiuh* means it will come to emerge. That is to say, it is even as the sun, which sometimes comes forth in great splendor; it comes, it quickly sets; no more is it thus splendid; it is what has vanished, what has corrupted. Nevermore comes he who has died. No more is he good who has been disgraced.

HE MOVETH THE SUN FORWARD A LITTLE

That is to say, he becomes a small child. The old men [and] the old women say: "Perhaps the small child is our desert, perhaps he is our merit"; or, "He will move the sun forward just a little."

I PLACE THE SUN IN THE MIDDLE

That is to say, I become a youth or I become a mature man; I am a marriageable young man. The saying says: "Such is his day sign; in such a time was N. born. He will place the sun in the middle." That is to say, he is the one who will soon die, who will not grow old.

THE SUN GOETH FALLING; OR I GO CAUSING THE SUN TO SET

That is to say, I am already an old man; I am already an old woman.

THE SUN HATH FALLEN, OR SET; AND IT IS SAID, "IT HATH DARKENED"

That is to say, he is already very old; he has grown very old. And it means that there is no need for him at all, as he is already as old as if he had died.

THE GOD IS EATEN; THERE IS AN EARTHQUAKE

"The god" means the sun.

That is to say, something terrifying comes to pass — perhaps war, perhaps the death of the ruler.

NOW THE SUN IS OVERTURNED

That is to say, a ruler is dead, or a city is destroyed; or a good custom disappears; or a wise man dies.

THE SUN GOETH FEEBLY

That is to say, the sun does not shine; there is no heat; the sun's rays are not warm; it remains cloudy.

toani omic opoliuh. anoço oavilquiz. in iuhqui q̃lli tlamanitiliztli opoliuh. yn anoço necuiltonolli opoliuh. anoçe callj.

in xiuh. q. n. texotic chimal. q. n. chimalli. quitoznequi yavaltic. tonati q. n. tonatiuh. momanaquiuh. q. n. quiçaq̃uh quitoznequi. In iuh tonatiuh quẽmã valquiça yn cẽca mavizyoh i vitz ỹ caletiuitz. ca aocmo ceppa iuh mavizyovaz yn tleĩ opoliuh. ỹ tlein ohitlacauh. aocmo ceppa vitz ỹ omic. aocmo ceppa qualtia ỹ oavilquiz.

ACHI QUIVALLALIA TONATIUH.

q. n. piltontli mochiva. quitoa ỹ veve in ilama. Aço tocnopil aço aço tomaceval ỹ piltzintli. anoço çã achi quiuallaliz tonatiuh.

NEPANTLA NICTLALIA Y TONATIUH.

q. n. nitelpuchtli ninochiva. anoço yyolloco noquichtli ninochiva nitlapaliui. quitoa in tlatolli iuhqui itonal yuhcan tlacat ỹ N. ỹ nepãtla quivallaliz tonatiuh q. n. ỹ çan cuel miquiz ỹ amo veuetiz.

ONVETZTIUH Ỹ TONATIUH. ANOÇO NOCONAQUIUHTIUH Ỹ TONATIUH.

q. n. ye niveve ye nilama.

OONVETZ Ỹ TONATIUH. ANOÇO OONAC. YOÃ MITOA OYOVAC.

quitoznequi. ye vel veue. ovelveuetic yoã quitoznequi. aoctle ynecoca inic ye veve iuhquin omic.

TEVTL QUALO TLALLOLINI.

ỹ teutl. quitoznequi tonatiuh

q. n. hitla temamauhti mochiva. aço yaoyotl. aço tlatocamiquiliztlj.

AXCÃ MIXTLAPACHMANA Ỹ TONATIUH.

q. n. tlatocamicoa anoço poliui ỹ altepetl. anoço qualli tlamanitiliztlj poliui. anoço tlamatini miqui.

ÇÃ COCOXTIUH Y TONATIUH.

q. n. amo tona amo tlatotonia amo totonqui yn tonalli mimixtẽtoc. auh in icaq'ztica quitoznequi.

And [as for] its significance, it means that life does not become strong; the ruler is not strong. Though he does a little good, yet it comes to pass that he is not strong.

amo chicava ỹ nemiliztli. amo chicavac ỹ tlatoani. tel achi qualli ỹ mochiva yeceh amo chicavac.

PERHAPS THE SUN WILL YET COME TO EMERGE; OR PERHAPS THE SUN WILL NOT EMERGE

It means a little ridicule. It indicates something new which is to happen which has never come to pass, like a miracle. [It is] as if it were said: "If thou dost this, I shall give thee a horse." He speaks, he answers [what is in the heading].

HACAÇOC OMPÃ QUIÇAQUIUH TONATIUH. ANOÇO. ACAÇOCMO OMPA VALQUIÇAZ TONATIUH.

quitoznequi. achi tenavallavaliztli. quinezcayotia. hitla yancuic mochiva. ỹ aic omochiuh ỹ iuhquima tlamaviçolli. In iuh mitoa Intla ticchivaz y. centetl Cauallo nimitzmacaz. quitoa tlananquilia

PERHAPS THE SUN WILL YET EMERGE THERE. YEA, VERILY

That is to say, "How wilt thou do that when thou hast never done it, and it is not known wherewith thou wilt do it? So a great miracle will come to pass?" That is to say, it is not my merit, it is not my desert. And it means, "Thou art poor."

ACAÇOC OMPA Ỹ VALQUIÇAZ TONATIUH TLA NELLI.

quitoznequi quenin ticchivaz ho yn aic oticchiuh. ỹ amo no nemacho hica ticchivaz. anca vei tlamaviçolli mochivaz. quitozneq' ca amo nolvil ca amo nomaceval. yoã quitozneq̃. ca titzotzoca.

VERILY, THE SUN DOTH NOT YET COME FORTH FROM THERE

That is to say, perhaps his failure is very great. He has no equal. Perhaps also the sun will be affronted. Perhaps it will no longer be strong there where it emerges from its place of emerging. That is to say, although one is valued, although one is great, there must needs be punishment. [But] when it must needs be, one need not therefore be ruined. For there will be living; for the world will endure; for the sun will shine; it will dawn.

TLA NELLI Ỹ MACA OC OMPA VALQUIÇA TONATIUH.

q. n. cuix cẽca vei in itlacaviz. çã nimã aoc tle inamic cuix no moyolitlacoz in tonatiuh cuix aocmo motlapaloz in ompa valquiçaz yquiçaya. q. n. Immanel tlaçotli ymmanel vei. monequi tlatzacuiltiloz in iquac monequi ca amo ipãpa tlatlacaviz. ca nemoaz. ca maniz in cemanavatl ca tonaz ca tlatviz.

VERILY, THE SUN WILL NOT YET EMERGE FROM THERE[177]

It means the same thing.

TLA NELLI Ỹ MACA OC OMPA QUIÇAQUI TONATIUH

çã no yehoatl quitoznequi.

TRULY THOU HAST ATTAINED THE SUN

That is to say, this same is required when you have deserved, have merited that which is very precious.

VEL TONATIUH Y OTICACIC.

q. n. vel yehoatl ỹ monequi ỹ otiquicnopilvi ỹ oticmaceuh. vellaçotli.

O SUN! THAT IS, O NANAUATL!

[Nanauatl] is said to be the sun. When there was not yet a sun, it is said there was little Nanauatl.

TONATIUE. Q. N. NANAVATLE.

quilmach ỹ tonatiuh. ỹ ayamo tonatiuh quil nanavaton catca.

LITTLE MOON DID NOT EXERT HIMSELF

That is to say, he who strives to do something which is difficult, which is great, which is beyond

HAMO YEYECO Ỹ METZPIL.

quitoznequi. In aquin hitla quichivaznequi ỹ vvih ỹ vei in iixco yeva in avel quichiva in aṭ noço ça vel

177. *quiçaqui*: read *quiçaquiuh*.

him, cannot do it; or else he can do it [but] only thereby dishonors himself; only thereby his renown is destroyed; as [if] he pursued rulership, or initiated a war; or tried to learn something.

quichiva ỹ çan ic mavilquixtia yn çã ic mavizyopoliui. In iuhqui tlatocayotl quitotoca. ỹ anoço yaoyotl quiyocaya. yn anoço hitla momachiznequi

This is its story. It is said that when the god was made, when the god was formed, in the time of darkness, it is said, there was fasting for four days. It is said that the moon would be the sun. And when four days were completed, it is said, the god was made during the night. And it is said that when the moon would be the sun, it is said, a very great fire was laid in the place called the gods' hearth, the turquoise enclosure.

In içaçanillo hi. quil yn iquin teutivac ỹ teutivaya yn yovayan. quil navilhuitl ỹ neçavaloc. quilmach yehoatl tonatiuh yezquia ỹ metztli. auh in oacic navilhuitl quil yovaltica ỹ teutiuac. auh quilmach hiquac tonatiuhtizquia ỹ metztli. quil cẽca vei ỹ tletl motlali ỹ mitoa tevtlecuilco in xiuhtetzaqualco.

And when it was already time for the god to be made, there was laid the very great fire into which was to leap, was to fall the moon — where he was to gain renown, glory; by which he would become the sun. And the moon thereupon went in order to leap into the fire. But he did not dare to do it; he feared the fire. Then all the gods shouted; they said: "When [is this to be], O gods? Let the sun stop!" But little Nanauatl[178] had already dared; he thereupon had leaped into the fire. Thus he became the sun.

auh ỹ ye ymma ỹ teutiuaz. omotlali in cẽca huei tletl in õcã oncholoz ỹ oncã onvetziz ỹ metztli yn õca quicuiz tleyotl mavizyotl inic tonatiuhtiz. Auh ỹ metztli nimã ye ic yauh in tleco choloz. Auh inic ye amo tlapaloa. quimacaz in tletl. Nimã tzatzique in ixquichtin teteu. quitoq'. quemmaya teteuye. tla vecava yn tonatiuh. Auh in navatõ ye motlapalo. ye õcholo in tleco. ynic yehoatl tonatiuh mochiuh.

And the moon, when he was deprived of the renown, the glory, was much shamed. Yet again he dared; he leaped into the fire. However, he only went to fall into the ashes.

Auh in metztli ỹ oõcuililoc yn tleyotl ỹ mavizyotl cẽca pinavac. ça oc ceppa motlapalo õcholo in tleco. yece çã nextitlã in vetzito.

There he lay only shamed; there he was struck repeatedly in the face with a rabbit. Hence it is said there is already [a rabbit] in his face. Now he is no longer warm; nor does his heat radiate.

çã õpa valpinauhtiloc ça õpa tochin ic valixtlatlahvitecoc ye in iixco cah axcan ic aocmo totonqui aocmo no tlanextia in itonallo.

This was said of him who ardently desired a thing yet did not so attain it.

Ic ipã mitoa ỹ aquĩ cẽtlamãtli cõmonectia çã yeh amo iuhqui ỹ quinamiqui

End of the First Book
Fray Bernardino de Sahagún

fin del prjmero libro
fray bernardino de sahagun

178. *navato*: read *nanauaton.*